MAKING NEW WORLDS

MAKING NEW WORLDS
The Way of the Artist

John C. Woodcock

iUniverse LLC
Bloomington

MAKING NEW WORLDS
The Way of the Artist

iUniverse books may be ordered through booksellers or by contacting:

iUniverse LLC
1663 Liberty Drive
Bloomington, IN 47403
www.iuniverse.com
1-800-Authors (1-800-288-4677)

ISBN: 978-1-4917-1776-9 (sc)
ISBN: 978-1-4917-1777-6 (e)

Printed in the United States of America.

iUniverse rev. date: 12/10/2013

CONTENTS

Permissions vii

Introduction ix

Art and Our Way of Being 1

Fictional Reality and Empirical Reality 11

Interpenetration of Realities 23

The Violent Character of the New "Art Form" 35

Towards a New World-Disclosing Language 47

What Kind of World? 55

The Marginal Practice: some examples 65

    • *Lighthouse at the End of the World* 67

    • *The Coming Storm* 81

    • *Sewing His Own Garment* 99

    • *Ur-Image* 135

    • *The Herm* 141

About the Author 151

Index 153

Bibliography 159

End Notes 165

i am a thief

i live in between

the road is my home

hodus

there is madness in my method

where others see throw-away

i see

windfall

theft

gift

revelation

i am . . .

world-discloser

PERMISSIONS

Cover	*Making New Worlds.* John C Woodcock (Adobe Photoshop).
Figure 1	*Herm with erect phallus.* Marble, ca. 520 BC. From Siphnos. Ricardo André Frantz (User:Tetraktys), 2006. http://en.wikipedia.org/wiki/File:0007MAN-Herma.jpg. Wikimedia Commons.
Figure 2	*Light of the World.* Holman Hunt: photo by Author.
Figure 3	*Brandung.* by lassedesignen @ Fotolia: www.us.fotolia.com.
Figure 4	*Thunderstorm.* Anna Langover: https://publicdomainpictures.net/view-image.php?image=2293 3&picture=thunderstorm.
Figure 5	*St. Matthew and the Angel.* Mikey Angels. http://en.wikipedia.org/wiki/File:Michelangelo_Merisi_da_Caravaggio_-_St_Matthew_and_the_Angel_-_WGA04127.jpg. Wikimedia Commons.
Figure 6	*Medusa.* Nicolas Pioch. http://en.wikipedia.org/wiki/file:medusa_by_carvaggio.jpg. Wikimedia Commons.
Figure 7	*New Pieta.* personal photo of sculpture by Fenwick Lawson. http://www.fenwicklawson.co.uk/. Permission granted.
Figure 8	*La Pieta. Michaelangelo.* Stanislav Traykov. http://en.wikipedia.org/wiki/File:Michelangelo%27s_Pieta_5450_cropncleaned.jpg. Wikimedia Commons.
Figure 9	*Lascaux Cave Painting.* Jack Versloot. http://en.wikipedia.org/wiki/File:Lascaux_II.jpg. Wikimedia Commons.

Figure 10 *Angelus Novus.* Paul Klee. http://www.inicia.es/de/m_cabot/paul_klee.htm @ http://en.wikipedia.org/wiki/File:Klee,_Angelus_novus.png. Wikimedia Commons.

Figure 11 *Hexagram. The Wanderer.* By author.

Figure 12 *Tailor.* Family photo owned by author.

Figure 13 *Abstract swirling vortex.* © L. Shat and Newgrange © Tetastock: Fotolia.com.

Figure 14 *Herm with erect phallus.* Marble, ca. 520 BC. From Siphnos. Ricardo André Frantz (User:Tetraktys), 2006. http://en.wikipedia.org/wiki/File:0007MAN-Herma.jpg. Wikimedia Commons.

Figure 15 *Author.* John C. Woodcock.

John C. Woodcock

In November 2013, Sydney hosted an annual festival called Dangerous Ideas. I was watching a segment on TV which featured three young people who employed an interesting artistic conceit in order to present their version of dangerous ideas. They imaginatively placed themselves in the year 2033 and reported back to us, here in 2013, how the world would have developed over the intervening twenty years. Each speaker began with current real trends in the political, environmental, scientific, and other domains, and then extrapolated them to give us a picture of the future, as if it had already happened. Each of the three pictures was optimistic: the climate-change movement was successful; energy sources had finally shifted to "clean sources"; the excesses of international corporations had stopped, and so on. The point of the exercise was to generate an image of a future, based on current trends, if we now acted upon them. The choice of trends was intended to generate hope, and then action on our part to bring about the imagined outcomes.

There a number of considerations regarding the future implicitly argued in such a presentation. The most important one is the methodology of attaining the projected future outcome. This methodology is brought into sharp focus in sports psychology. Top athletes are taught how to generate and stabilize an image of a favourable outcome, *as already attained*, and then to attain it through the exercise of mental and physical discipline. This is a highly successful methodology in sports that involve high stress and big rewards and the three festival speakers appear to have something like this in mind in their attempt to shape the future.

There are several difficulties here in this methodology. To imagine the future in the way the speakers did, choices have to be made concerning which current trend to extrapolate—choices that clearly support the prejudices of the speakers, as in my example here. Not everyone wants a world like that of the speakers, by any means. Not everyone wants even to base their current actions on such an imagined world of the future. For example, governments like that of the USA base their very real and consequential foreign policy actions, not on a "green outcome" but on a "worst case scenario" generated from present trends. Even if certain chosen trends were acted upon by many people, there is no way that any outcome can be predicted from our present actions any more than an athlete can guarantee success. There is just too much uncertainty. At most such methodologies simply generate hope, for a while.

A recent movie emerged (October 2013) that takes this methodology to its logical and absurd limit. Gravity is a film in which: [1]

> Dr. Ryan Stone is a Mission Specialist on her first space shuttle mission aboard the Space Shuttle Explorer. She is accompanied by veteran astronaut Matt Kowalski, who is commanding his final expedition . . . . Mission Control in Houston warns the team that space debris from a Russian missile strike on a defunct satellite has caused a chain reaction of destruction and that they must abort the mission. . . .

From this point on, the heroine is subjected to a series of catastrophes until she finally manages to return safely to earth. Throughout the movie she maintains the hope of returning to earth against incredible odds, with one lapse into suicidal despair which is quickly countered by her dead colleague showing her yet another faint possibility for getting back. The plot absurdly portrays the supremacy of hope in relation to an imagined future (returning home) over what would otherwise been judged accurately simply as impossible odds. The movie was released just at the time that the US Government ended a shutdown, narrowly averting default on its accumulated debts. But the crisis was merely put off until January the next year (2014). President Obama said that the US Government should "get out of the habit of governing by crisis". The hope-laden rhetoric in the media is exactly what the movie portrays so starkly: we *can* make it back from a $16 trillion national debt level if we act now. Meanwhile catastrophe after catastrophe continues to pummel the US economy.

Imagining this or that future as a way of generating hope and "hopeful action", far from moving us towards any desired outcome is simply occluding our eyes from the reality that is right in front of us, daily. Our time is incredibly uncertain and our lives are dominated by catastrophic thinking, with fear more and more determining our real actions and outcomes, on the local or world scale. The three presenters at the Festival of Dangerous Ideas were trying to combat this overwhelming tsunami of fear by generating hope, and the movie, *Gravity*, similarly wants to show that hope can, after all, win through even in the face of clearly impossible odds. As the General Accounting Office of the USA states, the level of debt sustained by the USA is in fact, unsustainable.

If we, finally, drop all pretence that hope can have any bearing on the future, we must then face the level of fear running freely through world affairs today and equally we must face the fact that predictability is impossible in regards to the future. We must face that we are "in between worlds". By this I mean that a former way of being has come to an end and a new way of being has yet to be configured. Thus we live in chaos.

Under these circumstances we can ask: is there any adequate way of addressing the future at all: a way that does not blind us to the fearful realities of our present times; a way that does not address the unknown future in terms of predictability or hope; a way that nonetheless may indeed help prepare the unknown future? [2]

There is, and I will call it the way of the "artist". [3]

Let's begin with Heidegger.

ART AND OUR WAY OF BEING

[U]nfamiliar moments, such as anxiety or joy, provide the deepest illumination. Such moments are "pre-worldly": they have not yet been articulated into patterns of significations. "Pre-worldly" moments are founts of meaning, generating systems of sense yet irreducible to these systems.

Richard Polt

I was led to a study of Heidegger through an experience that I believe suggests his concept of Ereignis. [4] Richard Polt's thorough study of this difficult Heideggerian concept shows that, over his life-time, Heidegger was attempting to approach, not any particular way of being or life-world, but the specific moment that a life-world becomes established in the first place.[5] Since language and ways of being are intimately related, any attempt to put into words the movement that establishes a way of being or world is exceedingly difficult. As Polt says, "Such thinking cannot simply present a disengaged report on Ereignis, but must take part in it and flow from it". Polt also offers a vivid image that may help us:[6]

> Heidegger eventually claims that even the general experience that "there is something" can be a genuine Ereignis—and even a sign of "the highest potentiality of life". It can happen in "gliding from one world of experience to another genuine life-world, or in moments of especially intensive life . . . As a case of "life-intensity" we might think of an artistic breakthrough in which a poet or painter experiences the sheer wonder that there is something instead of nothing. As a case of "gliding" between life-worlds, consider the moment in which one returns from a long trip and settles back into one's house. For an hour or so there is an opportunity to see home with new eyes and to experience oneself neither as traveler nor as resident but as "someone" unsettled, encountering "something" unsettled. Such an experience is still one's own, but who one is has temporarily become a problem.

Polt here is describing a moment of inception, a "pre-world encounter", "a unique eruption of meaning", or an "artistic breakthrough" where one way of being gives way to another (in *status nascendi*). His delightful, not uncommon, example of a traveller returning home, "unsettled", seeing the once-familiar world with fresh eyes and therefore, for a moment, sensing the presence of a world (rather than simply taking it for granted, as we normally do) suggests the meaning of Ereignis as may occur to an "artist".

In the Introduction, I proposed that we are now living in a time that is between worlds, a time of chaos. In the light of this suggestion, Polt's description of Ereignis becomes essential today for understanding the way of the "artist" as a practice for preparing the unknown future, just as Heidegger felt it to be essential in his own time (of the Nazi regime).[7] Implicit in Polt's discussion of Ereignis is another very difficult thought. If we are talking about the establishment of a world, or new way of being, then we are not merely talking about the "artist" gaining fresh perceptions of the facts of the same old world, we are, astoundingly, talking about a new world with a new set of facts. With Ereignis, the *facts* transform.

We are fortunate enough to have accounts of such "world disclosing events":[8]

> We walked down the path to the well-house, attracted by the fragrance of the honeysuckle with which it was covered. Someone was drawing water and my teacher placed my hand under the spout. As the cool stream gushed over one hand she spelled into the other the word "water" first slowly, then rapidly. i [sic] stood still, my whole attention fixed upon the motion of her fingers. Suddenly i felt a misty consciousness as of something forgotten—a thrill of returning thought; and somehow the mystery of language was revealed to me. i knew then that "w-a-t-e-r" meant the wonderful cool something that was flowing over my hand. That living word awakened my soul, gave it light, joy, set it free! . . . i left the well-house eager to learn. Everything had a name, and each name gave birth to a new thought. As we returned to the house each object that i touched seemed

to quiver with life. That was because i saw everything with the strange new light that had come to me.

In this evocative example of inception, Helen Keller established a new world that simultaneously became disclosed to her, a new way of being. The incursion of fresh meaning appeared as a light by which she could see the new facts. This event clearly demonstrates the "pre-world phenomenology" of Ereignis.

Owen Barfield pays close attention to this process of inception in his book, *Saving the Appearances*:[9]

> Men concerned with the development of any branch of thought, if they happen also to be acutely conscious of the workings of their own minds, are sometimes surprised at the ease and force with which ideas tending in some direction have come into them.

Barfield then goes on to quote John Stuart Mill who reports such an experience while reading a text: "The feeling rushed upon me . . . that here was the commencement of a new era in thought."

Henri Bortoft gives us another compelling example that further specifies how Ereignis establishes a new world, in the historical example of Galileo:[10]

> [I]t is reported that Galileo made a telescope, and that when he looked through it he saw mountains and valleys on the moon, as if this knowledge came to him down the telescope and through his eyes. The account which Galileo himself gave of his observations with the telescope makes it quite clear that to begin with he saw nothing of the kind.

Bortoft tells us that Galileo simply saw blotches until, and this is the crucial creative act of inception, an inrush of meaning occurred which Galileo perceived in its forming, or coming into being. This enlivened "creative thinking" only subsequently became the new sensory data which everyone else could then see as the mountains and valleys of the moon. A new world was born: the moon that once appeared as the gate for departing souls now appeared, as it now does for us, as an empirical reality, like earth, with no spiritual connotations. The facts have changed. We enter a new world.

Obviously Galileo did not create this new world of positivism or empirical reality single-handedly. If "world" is to mean anything it must mean a public, shared reality. His contemporary, Descartes, also contributed to this world by his formulation of a private inner world set against an outer non-mental world. Even as early as 400 AD, Augustine suggested that we "possess" an inner life by pointing out that we do not have to read out aloud: "but when he was reading, his eye glided over the pages, and his heart searched out the sense, but his voice and tongue were at rest."[11]

In Heidegger's terms, with reference to art as that which configures a new world, Galileo, Descartes, and Augustine were engaging in "marginal practices", which later gathered (contingently) into a new central style, or way of being—a new world.

Hubert Dreyfus introduces the relationship between marginal practices (or scattered practices) and life-worlds this way:[12]

> Works of art can show us a new way of understanding what is important and trivial, central and marginal, to be ignored or demanding of our attention and concern. They do this by giving us a work which can serve as a cultural paradigm. As such, the work shapes a culture's sensibilities by collecting the scattered [marginal] practices of a people, unifying them into coherent and meaningful possibilities for action, and epitomizing this unified and coherent meaning in a visible fashion. The people, in turn, by getting in tune with the artwork,

can then relate to each other in the shared light of the work. As we become attuned to the sense for the world embodied by a work of art, our ways of being disposed for everything else in the world can change also.

Dreyfus is saying here that the many "marginal practices" that individuals are engaged in, none of which alone constitute a new paradigm, can gather into a work that does indeed manifest, articulate, or reconfigure the style of a culture, disclosing for us the new world in which we live.[13]

In this regard I think of Picasso's *Minotauromachy* as such a work of art. He shows the Minotaur approaching, or bursting into the town (civilization) producing panic and destruction. Perhaps starting with Nietzsche's insight into modernity's will-to-power, we can see such thought and its many variations gathered together in a beautiful, compelling, and very disturbing picture of our world today—a world of terror and panic, as a "brute" force approaches human awareness. The only figure standing in its way is a young girl holding flowers and a candle—a precarious situation at best. It suggests to me a world in which we are meeting a fresh incursion of Power with a kind of youthful innocence or naiveté; or, maybe, Picasso is also showing us an image of fictional reality penetrating into empirical reality, a penetration for which we are quite unprepared.

This process of manifesting, articulating, or reconfiguring the style of a culture (life-world) is characteristic of Heidegger's understanding of how new worlds come into being. It therefore is very disturbing to read his understanding of some unique features of our times that may, for the first time in history, inhibit any possibility of any new configuration emerging from within our present culture. His arguments are complex and involved but something needs to be said here in order to indicate the difficulty for those modern "artists" engaged in marginal practices in getting any hearing at all.

Heidegger appeals to the historical capacity of "things" to gather around them what he calls the "the fourfold": earth, sky, divinity, mortals.[14] Put briefly this difficult schema seems to me to point to how things once could appear, not merely as isolated objects, but as imbued with meaning that could disclose an entire world that gave rise to the presence of the thing in the first place.[15] I was once given some nails, made in the early 20th C. They were hand-made and each one was individual. For a few minutes a world awakened for me, a world of tradesmen, handicrafts, cottages, the smell of leather, the heat of the furnace, the reality of matter from which the nail was drawn, the striving towards a meaningful future (to live according to god's will, etc), all revealing for a moment, the tradesman's efforts in coming into conformity with seasons and cycles of nature, cultural beliefs, etc.

In our technological civilization, however, the "things" no longer gather such conditions for their very presence as what they are any more. Things have become resources, replaceable and meaningless. Heidegger saw a kind of flattening take place, where the "conditions" or the four-fold that gives meaning to the "things", is now totally occluded, presenting any reconfiguration in our way of being from taking place. We could say, in simpler terms, that today we live on the surface of life. The inwardness or depth of life is now totally occluded from our vision. In order to reconfigure the world, we need access to that depth and inwardness, since that is the "source" of, or maybe is, Ereignis, the inception, or inrush of meaning, that alters the facts and discloses a new world.

Those individuals, who are presently engaged in marginal practices, are thus faced with the problem of expressing fresh meaning from within the presently configured world that, by its linguistic nature, excludes anything other than surface or literal meaning. Heidegger's response to this "technological" dilemma seems to have been a call for the preservation of "pre-technological practices that remain in our culture so that one day they may come together in a new work of art, rich enough and resistant enough to reconfigure our world."[16] This approach is taken up by Dreyfus and Polt but both authors give examples that seem to me to be a form of make-believe, i.e., they each advocate marginal practices that merely imitate (our idea of), or play-act, past worlds. For example Polt:[17]

> For many of us now who find that the conservation of natural things makes sense, the most primordial way of responding to them is in terms of practices attached to old pantheistic ways of seeing things. For under this view, all natural things seem worthy of celebration, and this yearning for celebration awakens us to our ecological way of life.

And Dreyfus:[18]

> [P]erhaps our marginal practices could gather into a new style, one, for example, in which marginal practices and attunements like awe in the face of nature from our pre-Socratic past would begin to coalesce with the nature worship of the Romantics to affirm what is sometimes referred to as the Gaia Principle, i.e. that nature is god. Perhaps then some new paradigm would make those marginal practices central and marginalize our current practices, which, as Heidegger once put it, "are turning the earth into a gigantic filling station."

Such suggested marginal practices are simply nostalgic! The fact is that today, we comport ourselves in a world that is positivist in its character. The "things" (natural things, like animals, plants etc., or technological things) no longer "speak". We all know this fact. We comport ourselves accordingly and thus disclose the positivist world we inhabit. I remember a colleague of mine who shares Polt's and Dreyfus' nostalgic longings for past life-worlds. He was leading a group in which he intended to teach, or initiate, others into the reality of Gaia today, "living nature"! He told them what to do. They were to go into nature and sit under a tree and wait for it to speak to them. He said this in all earnest and the other group members were already "on board" with the stated program. Yet, when he suggested this course of action, the group members gave out involuntary small embarrassed laughs, and so did he! This is the difference between believing and knowing. My colleague believed in Gaia but he, along with others, revealed what they really knew—no Gaia, no speaking trees, only dead exploitable nature belongs to our world today. The rest is play-acting, make-believe.

Although there are many similar marginal practices today, they cannot gather into a reconfiguration of our present world, as Dreyfus vainly hopes. Their time is over and we know it. A reconfiguration must arise from within our present configuration, as expressed by Heidegger:[19]

> What ultimately bestows the material for the new style is the style of a people's language. Art takes place in a clearing "which has already happened unnoticed in language".

Returning to past practices can never "take place in a clearing" etc. Only those marginal practices that are apprehending and rendering *new* movements within our modern language can become candidates for a new world configuration. As with any marginal practice throughout history, these "artists" will be poorly understood or even vilified, quite unlike practices that imitate the imagined past and which are well understood, praised, and even "believed in", leading to all sorts of anachronistic "ways of being".

With this background study of marginal practices and art as a way of configuring and illuminating a world, we are now in a position to explore those "artists" who are, in effect, becoming that clearing and participating with Ereignis—the inception of a new style of language that is the germ of a new world, arising from within, and transcending our present one (of positivism, or as Heidegger says, technological).[20]

FICTIONAL REALITY AND EMPIRICAL REALITY

The single most striking realization that Fat had come to was his concept of the universe as irrational and governed by an irrational mind, the creator deity. If the universe were taken to be rational, not irrational, then something breaking into it might seem irrational, since it would not belong. But Fat, having reversed everything, saw the rational breaking into the irrational. The immortal plasmate had invaded our world and the plasmate was totally rational, whereas our world is not.

Philip K. Dick

In order to get some hint of a marginal practice that may be "bestowed" as a new style, or at least the beginnings of one, we must notice that "which has already happened unnoticed in language", as Heidegger says above. No small task indeed! How can we notice the unnoticed? I believe this task lies in the hands of "artists"—those individuals whose eyes have been opened to the "unnoticed", and who then can thus perceive the beginnings of a new style, or new world, that is arising from within our current reality.

These artists must have some experience of a new way of being that arises from within and at the same time transcends our current reality. Before I give some examples of these experiences, we should attempt to give some adequate articulation of our current way of being, or reality. In my book, *Manifesting New Futures: Towards a New Genre of Literature*, I describe at length the evolution of reality as an increasing separation between "inner" and "outer", along with "sudden" transformations, culminating in a dichotomy between (what therefore has become) empirical reality and fictional reality. Empirical reality is now the true reality while fictional reality has been downgraded to, well, fiction, i.e., the not really real, or the unreal.[21]

This dichotomy has given us a world that is a world of surfaces only, the world of the literal. It is a world that we "look upon" from the outside as it were, with no depth to what we perceive, i.e., a depth of meaning that once surrounded us and determined our lives.

To give a taste of this momentous shift in our way of being, I explored, in the same book and chapter cited above, some historical literary sources that demonstrate the shift, unnoticed, in their language (i.e., implicit within the content of the story).[22]

I want to enrich these examples with an account of a shift, given by Wolfgang Giegerich, in which:[23]

the rugged mountains of the Alps caused sheer terror in the people of that age (17th C.) The very same sights that today attract millions of tourists were then experienced as horrifying. Even courageous men would not venture into the "desolate and wayless wilderness of forests and mountains" without necessity. In the reports of travelers to Italy who had to cross the Alps, we read how horror-stricken they were at the sight of gorges and cliffs.

A hundred years later the situation began to change as a result of the Enlightenment . . . Jean Jacques Rousseau, the French philosopher, describes in his autobiography that he loved to walk to his favorite place in the Savoyan Alps, a path at the edge of a ravine, where, secured by a railing, he could look down into the gorge . . . in order to procure the feeling of dizziness for himself at his ease, and he adds, "I love this whirling, provided that I am in safety."

As with the examples of historical literature in my book, we can sense an ontological (way of being) tectonic shift taking place between the 17th C. and 18th C. and on to today's world of empirical reality. In the 17th C., people felt themselves to be surrounded by nature, or embedded within it. When they gazed into the gorges of the Alps, they experienced terrifying and yet meaningful depths of being! The gorges had not yet become merely empirical; they had an "inner", an interiority that surrounded them at that time, inspiring awe.

Rousseau's account, on the other hand, displays a world in which that former immense and abysmal depth of being was beginning to be "fenced in", with us on the "outside" looking at it, no longer surrounded by its immensity. Accompanying this momentous shift was a kind of turning inside out of feeling. Where once foreboding, terror, danger, awe "belonged" to the gorge, or to nature, as its inner, we now became the possessors of this inwardness in the form of the "thrill", an inversion that gave birth to a genre of literature known as Sentimentalism, and later, Gothic literature. Nature thus became deprived of any "inner" as it became established as *our* "inner".

This newly acquired human "inner", i.e., the realm of images, became a source of fascination for us, particularly because inner images could be manipulated by us in order to induce the "thrill". The reality of the "inner", once feared and/or adored, assumed the ontological status of "the fabulous, the fictive, the imaginative, the invented, the feigned, and now, today, the fantastic"—in short: the unreal.[24]

The reality of what was once the "inner" of nature, that Being that surrounded us and determined our lives has now become utterly "fenced in" and rendered mute or innocuous. Obviously on an empirical level we are still impacted by natural events, but our way of being remains immune from any penetration from these events as happenings. Nature is no longer able to transform us or initiate us into the mysteries of Being, since it is now ontologically completely exploitable by us, for our own purposes.[25]

With this very brief discussion of the history of Being, leading to the current dichotomy between empirical reality (the really real) and fictional reality (the unreal) we are now in a position to ask if we can discern a "marginal practice" (Heidegger's possibility of a new style or new way of being) in the making, arising from within the current configuration of reality. Who are those "artists" whose eyes are opened up to a new reality though Ereignis, or inception?[26]

A book has recently been published (2009) which does indeed display such a marginal practice. It is a book that has produced much controversy and indeed, excitement, for a variety of reasons. To my knowledge, though, C. G. Jung's *Liber Novus* or *The Red Book* has not yet been examined in terms of its unique contribution to literature, as the seed of a new genre, expressive of a new way of being that arises from within our current reality and transcends it.

In short I will show here that the question of what kind of book is *The Red Book*—a question that vexed Jung for most of his life, along with commentators subsequent to its publication—arises only because we have not yet noticed that "which has already happened unnoticed in language". [27]

Shortly before his death in 2011, James Hillman held a series of conversations with Sonu Shamdasani regarding the perplexities of *The Red Book*. These conversations were subsequently published. [28] Both men speak of Jung's struggle to articulate a language that "evokes the poetic basis of mind" or allows the psyche to speak itself—a metaphorical language that gives voice to "the dead".

Jung famously denied that what he was doing during the creation of *The Red Book* is art. [29] Instead of simply producing art or revelations which speak for themselves, he seemed to be asking a new kind of question altogether: what is the psychological process by which art or revelation comes into existence: [30]

> **SS:** He's inventing the rules as he goes along. He's trying to find his way, trying to find what is right and fitting expression and what form that should take. So it's a linguistic experiment to find right and fitting expression that is reflecting back on a series of fantasies a year later and thinking, pondering the significance of his engagement. This is the reflective dimension of retrospective engagement.

> **JH:** But when a voice says to him "This is art" and he says "No, it's not art," although he's tempted, he's rejecting or he's realizing how close what he is doing is to what a musician or a composer must experience when a flood of music comes. He has to put it into a form, express it in the language of music. How do you express this in a language that's not art, not poetry, but in the language of psychology? Isn't that the reflection

that he's trying for? Or maybe not even in the language of psychology. How do you find the language for what's happening?

Shamdasani believes that Jung is actively engaging with the purely fictional figures that he encounters, and writing out the encounter as he goes along—a belief that I support from my own reading of *The Red Book*. Hillman seems similarly to believe, based on his own psychological project (Archetypal Psychology), that Jung is engaging the fictional characters as a fictional character himself—a process quite familiar to writers such as Lewis Carroll whose Alice, an ordinary little girl, enters fictional reality and works within its categories of experience. She engages the caterpillar, Mad Hatter, etc. completely on their terms, while in Wonderland.[31]

In support of Hillman's claim, Shamdasani offers a passage from *The Red Book* in which a figure (the serpent soul) speaks to Jung saying, "I give you payment in images."[32] This passage is meant to support the thesis that Jung's language is the language of image, of metaphor, the language of fictional reality. As the passage continues, Jung is presented with fictional figures such as Salome and, like Alice, he takes her completely seriously, on her own (fictional) terms. A long engagement follows between Salome and Jung's "I" which would seem to be an exemplary example of what Hillman means by "evoking a poetic basis of mind"—including an imaginal "I" which is simply one fictional figure among others.

There is a detail, however, that both Hillman and Shamdasani appear to overlook in their analysis of *The Red Book*. It is a detail that, once seen, reveals *The Red Book* not as a text that gives us a language that simply expresses the reality of image or fictional reality (as separate from empirical reality). It is a text that inaugurates an entirely new genre of literature. This genre expresses the inception of a new world in which our current one (empirical reality vs. fictional unreality) is overcome! This new world appears to be one in which fictional reality gains the same status of reality as empirical reality, and it does so by penetrating into empirical reality on an equal ontological footing, as it were—a startling and perplexing state of affairs as we shall see.

The detail that Hillman and Shamdasani overlook may be seen in the small quote from *The Red Book*: The fictional serpent says: "I give you payment *in images* [my italics]." This statement is peculiar because we have an image referring to images, as if the image (serpent) is simultaneously within fictional reality and outside it (i.e., in empirical reality where such a category of thought belongs— thinking about images rather than engaging them imaginally, like Alice did).

This is not the only example of such strangeness. To date it appears that only one analyst of *The Red Book* has noticed it—Wolfgang Giegerich.[33] In his own analysis of *The Red Book*, Giegerich presents several compelling examples of the same peculiar syntax in Jung's text. For example, when confronting two figures, Elijah and Salome, supposedly as the imaginal "I" that Hillman and Shamdasani believe, Jung says:[34]

> **I:** You, Elijah, who are a prophet, the mouth of God, and she, a bloodthirsty horror. You are a symbol of the most extreme contradiction.
>
> **E:** We are real and not symbols.

As Giegerich says, this strange syntax is as though a novel within itself tried to pull the rug out from under its characters as only imagined, or as if we, while dreaming, turned around to the wild animal or to the murderous criminal chasing us and said to them, "you are only symbols of my shadow."[35]

We can deepen our understanding of this perplexity by comparing it to the well-known genre of fiction that expresses and yet maintains the dichotomy between empirical reality and fictional reality (our current world today). Let's turn once again to Alice in Wonderland.

When Alice drops into Wonderland, she leaves the categories of thought that belong to empirical reality behind and becomes fictional herself (the imaginal "I"), evaluating this new reality within its own terms (remember her long conversations with the caterpillar and the Mad Hatter, for example).[36] While she is inside the fiction, i.e., as the imaginal "I", each character opens up to its own interiority and depth, its own truth. Although Alice is amazed and perturbed by the various characters, she does not question their reality, using empirical categories. While she is in Wonderland, they are as real as she is, demanding that they be taken on their own terms, which Alice does willingly. When she shrinks and grows large, she is frightened, yes, but not doubtful or sceptical. She simply deals with each situation, as the situation itself demands. If an opiate-smoking caterpillar talks to her, she simply engages with it as best she can, trying to understand it entirely from within the fiction. She refrains from making the claim that the caterpillar, for example, could not exist because caterpillars do not smoke opium and cannot talk.

When she does at the end finally employ an empirical category of thought, "O, you all are just a pack of cards!" she moves out of fictional reality back into empirical reality where she becomes a little girl once more (she wakes up from a dream). You could say that Alice's employing that empirical category of thought is the very logical means by which she moves out of fictional reality back into empirical reality. We do the same every morning that we wake up out of a dream-state with an exclamation: "Whew, what a dream!"

The text of Alice's adventures displays a structure of world in which an empirical/fictional separation is maintained. This historically determined separation emerged with the scientific revolution, empirical reality being privileged as reality, and imaginal reality being downgraded to, well, fiction, the unreal!

The text of Jung's book, on the other hand, shows something very strange happening—historically unheard-of.

"Jung's account" is the account given by an ego that, from the start, is logically exterior to the fictional images and thus could call them psychic facts, a description only possible to a consciousness for which empirical reality is the privileged reality. So far, Jung is on the same level of logical structure as Lewis Carroll.

The difference between Jung's text and that of Carroll's emerges when we note how Alice enters the fictional world by passively falling down the rabbit hole (she falls asleep), leaving the empirical world behind. Jung, on the other hand, in a deliberate and programmatic move, forces his way into the fictional, while leaving his categories of empirical reality intact.[37]

> I devised such a boring method [i.e. tunnelling] by fantasizing that I was digging a hole, and by accepting this fantasy as perfectly real. This is naturally somewhat difficult to do—to believe so thoroughly in a fantasy that it leads you into further fantasy, just as if you were digging a real hole . . .

Alice moves smoothly between empirical and fictional reality, as we do when we fall asleep and dream. Like Alice, we normally do not need to persuade ourselves about the reality of the dream while we are dreaming. Jung's approach to fictional reality however requires his having to accept it as real, i.e., he has to convince himself, and it is difficult to do so. There is a doubt in place throughout. We can also see that, while Jung is engaging as one image to another, as might happen in a dream, he at the same time is also evaluating or interpreting the image "from the outside", i.e., as an empirical ego would.

The unheard-of move by Jung is that he employs empirical categories of thought while remaining, by an act of will, within the imaginal state. "Disagreeable", "madness", "sceptical resistance", all evaluations made by Jung while encountering purely fictional characters, can be made only by an ego that has attained a form of consciousness we know as positivistic today, i.e., the modern empirical ego.[38]

But this is not all that is going on.

As I pointed out earlier, one of the intriguing details about Jung's methodology, in writing *The Red Book*, that commanded Hillman and Shamdasani's attention, is whether he wrote while experiencing his encounters or afterwards, upon reflection. In my view this is a critical detail. I believe there is sufficient evidence to indicate that Jung wrote while participating in the fictional realm, as an empirical ego.

In the following passage Jung is confronted, within fictional reality, by a murdered child and a woman standing by, whose face is covered by a veil. To his horror, the woman demands that he eat the liver of the child. He does so:[39]

> I kneel down on the stone, cut off a piece of the liver and put it in my mouth. My gorge rises—tears burst from my eyes—cold sweat covers my brow—a dull sweet taste of blood—I swallow with desperate efforts—it is impossible—once again and once again—I almost faint—it is done. The horror has been accomplished.

We are not here merely reading an imaginative account of what it would be like to eat the liver of a murdered little girl. As such we could compare this graphic description with many other, equally compelling, and perhaps even fascinating horror stories such as those by Edgar Allen Poe, or Dante's journey through Inferno.

We are instead witnessing a first-hand account of the actual experience of the empirical Jung while in the realm of fantasy.

Jung is not in the fantasy as an imaginal "I", as Dante was in *The Divine Comedy*, but as the empirical "I". *The Red Book* is analogous to reading a diary or a grotesque first-hand report of an actual act of cannibalism with the unheard-of twist that here, although Jung's reactions are empirical, the act is purely fictional! Moreover, this text suggests that, as well as Jung's "forcing his way" into fictional reality as an empirical ego, fictional reality itself was forcing itself "into" Jung. Empirical reality is here being penetrated by fictional reality. It appears that Jung is intending to produce a literary form that expresses this process of an interpenetration of fictional and empirical reality.

There is another compelling example of this process with which Jung participated.

He reports that on one occasion:[40]

> . . . I tried to follow the same procedure, but it would not descend. I remained on the surface. Then I realized I had a conflict within myself about going down, but I could not make out what it was [the conflict then appeared to Jung as an image of two serpents fighting, one retired defeated and the fantasy then deepened] . . . I saw the snake approach me . . . the coils reached up to my heart. I realized as I struggled, that I had assumed the attitude of the Crucifixion. In the agony and the struggle, I sweated so profusely that the water flowed down on all sides of me . . . I felt my face had taken on the face of an animal of prey, a lion or a tiger.

These reports come subsequent to the writing of *The Red Book* and as such are memories of Jung's experience yet they seem to me to be memories of the same interpenetration of fictional and empirical realities.[41]

John C. Woodcock

In my book, *Manifesting Futures: towards a new genre of literature*, I explore further distinctions between established genres and what seems here to be Jung's "marginal practice" in Heidegger's sense, i.e., a practice that could lead to an art form that actually reconfigures and manifests our understanding of a new way of being, i.e., a new world.[42]

Can we find further evidence of such a marginal practice elsewhere, now that our eyes have been opened to the interpenetration of realities taking place in Jung's book?

Are other people having these kinds of experiences?

My eyes were opened to Jung's marginal practice when, over a twenty-year period, I also encountered purely fictional figures who had an initiatory effect on me in my empirical reality. During this ordeal I was taken to the edge of madness:[43]

> For weeks I experienced a flooding of my body with a kind of nectar that produced an ecstasy in me. I could smell flowers or sweet fragrance in the air. I felt I had grown a pair of wings, palpably, concretely. The erotic intensity was such that I would lay down for hours as a fount of glorious liquid fire poured into me. Many dreams came, and visions, too many to recount here but the flood swept away everything that I had so far assumed about Life, the human condition and its limitations. I was given experiences of a concrete nature, whose reality could not be questioned at all and yet which could not possibly be reduced or interpreted back into known categories of experience.
>
> These experiences thus have to stand on their own—incontrovertible proof of a reality, discrete yet interpenetrating with ordinary reality. At the peak of my ecstasies, I met a being who I called my beloved Star Sister. She came to me while I was fully awake, alone in my bed. I could get out of bed and see quite clearly with my outer vision that I was alone yet I also saw, felt, and touched her there beside me, as real as my knowledge that I was alone. Both realities were interpenetrating each other. It was then that I experienced myself as being loved by another, totally as an object of divine desire. Here I learned that the human body is able to receive an influx of love from the Beyond. It is the organ of the heart that is the door and it is the self-imposed limitations of the ego that close the door. I felt fearful that I could not contain it and was told again and again by my divine lover that I could, that I needed only to

open up completely, right to the level of the cells of
my body. I discovered that I could do this and in that
condition of complete surrender I received the poetry
that came to me.

These experiences led to an out-pouring of "poetry"—language
that expressed the reality or world that was disclosing itself to
me. It came into being as it was disclosed. Since that time (1994)
I have simply refined my understanding of this new world as my
marginal practice. Like Hermes I have shamelessly thieved language
from others but always in the spirit of "inventiveness and animated
swiftness" moving ahead "by leaps and bounds", as theft and
windfall unite in producing an act of transformation.[44] Further
examples of this interpenetration of realities may be found in my
book, *The Imperative.*[45]

These life-changing experiences were disturbing in Heidegger's
sense of generating tremendous anxiety—an existential anxiety
or unsettledness that occurred when my previous way of being
(empirical reality) no longer held any intrinsic or absolute meaning.
Over time I began to understand that I was going through a kind of
apocalypse, the end of one world and the emergence of another, as
yet unformed or stable. The dichotomous reality that is our present
world (empirical reality vs. fictional unreality) is breaking down and
a new reality formed from their interpenetration is emerging, albeit
as a marginal practice at this stage.[46]

As well as working for years simply to articulate my own version
of this transformation, I began to look around with my "new eyes"
to see if others too, are undergoing this apocalypse, no doubt
with similar disorienting effects. Jung's autobiography, *Memories,
Dreams, Reflections* offered tantalizing hints of his "confrontation
with the unconscious", as he calls it but I had to wait until 2009
when *The Red Book* was published to get what seems to me to be
clear evidentiary support for what I was trying to articulate.[47]

There are others, too.

For example, a world-wide movement called The International Community for Hearing Voices is now in its 14th year, while another, the Hearing Voices Network is in its 26th year (2013).[48] [49]

These movements grew out of an astonishing re-evaluation of the nature of hallucinations by some in the psychiatric community. The medical and psychiatric community almost universally regards non-ordinary experiences such as hearing voices, visions, tactile or olfactory hallucinations, as a sign of schizophrenia. The content or reality status of the experience is of no interest to the medical practitioner. Instead the therapeutic goal is to "normalize" the patient by eliminating the ego-alien intrusion. The dreadful side effects of powerful medications and the social stigma attached to the diagnosis have left many patients more isolated than ever from human community.

A tiny seed of change began in the Netherlands when a psychiatrist by the name of Marius Romme took an unprecedented step of shifting his focus from "voices-as-symptom" to simply "voices". In other words he took his patient seriously when she insisted that the only problem for her was the voices, not the schizophrenia.[50]

Today there are flourishing groups for Voice Hearers (note the non-pejorative term) all over the world because of this new appraisal and attitude towards fictional voices. For example Intervoice aims to:[51]

- show that hearing voices is a normal though unusual variation in human behavior;
- show that the problem is not hearing voices but the inability to cope with the experience;
- educate society about the meaning of voices so as to reduce ignorance & anxiety and to ensure this innovatory approach on voice hearing is better

known by voice hearers, families, professionals and
the general public;

- demonstrate the wide variety of voice hearing
  experiences and their origins, and peoples'
  approaches to coping;

- increase the quality and quantity of mutual support
  available to all people and organisations involved in
  hearing voices work across the world;

- make our work more effective and develop more
  non-medical ways of helping voice hearers cope
  with their experiences.

It seems that many people have such experiences today without
being diagnosed at all.[52]

In a democratic gesture the Hearing Voices Network argues for
meaning to emerge from the patient rather than imposing meaning
(diagnosis) from outside experts. Once found, this meaning can be
a life-long support and compass for the individual, helping her once
again connect with others in a community.

Research into these non-ordinary states of mind is also going on in
two broad fronts. Firstly, if the voices are not dismissed, but instead
taken seriously, researchers are asking how a loving community can
best support the individual in terms of functioning more adequately
in her life; secondly, research is exploring the nature, causes, and
origin of these voices.

As far as the second goal of the research goes, a good deal of interest
is going towards the connection between the appearance of voices
and trauma, particularly sexual trauma.[53]

This approach seems to seek the aetiology of ego-alien mental states
in actual traumatic events in the patient's life. Many hearers seem to
find solace in such explanations which do indeed tie disparate and

disjointed life "happenings" into a tapestry of sorts that one can live with and indeed others (family, friends etc.) can live with too.

Trauma is the going explanation for so many "clinical" conditions today that I would be hard pressed to enumerate them all but such an explanation at least does serve to bring one's "story" into alignment with the prevailing narratives that together constitute the modern world of pathology and health. Such an alignment in itself has healing value.

The fact that such explanations have this useful heuristic function does not mean that they are true! To get to the meaning or truth that lies deep within these strange experiences requires a method of research that stays faithful to the experiences and first hand narratives given by voice hearers and to enter those experiences deeply until the meaning is released. The Hearing Voices Network has begun this kind of research by the methodological stance of granting primacy to the actual experience of voices. But we need to go more deeply, rather than breaking off into sociological research (inquiries about actual past childhood experience etc.)

If we do this, we enter a very strange arena indeed. First we pay attention to the staggering numbers of people who are emerging into the light, now that stigma is reduced, to claim their status as voice hearers. Next there is a universal claim among hearers that the voices are real, as concretely real as you or me speaking, and as sensual as another person's body (smells, tastes, visions, voices . . .) The voices have a kind of independence, autonomy, and subjectivity, in the same way that empirical reality has, to date, appropriated to itself.

Yet many hearers would also acknowledge that the voices are also the hearer's own mind. This objective reality occurring within the hearer's own mind cannot be collapsed into an identity with ordinary outer reality without the danger of psychosis.

The two realities must thus be distinguished without reducing the reality status of either one! This distinction can be won for example by the hearer who challenges a voice to carry out a threat in outer reality (such as: "I can kill your parents"). When nothing happens, the hearer is in a position to distinguish the two realities, without devaluing either.

From this brief phenomenological investigation we are forced to articulate the following tentative meaning of the phenomenon of hearing voices today. I am advancing the hypothesis here, born out of the phenomenon of hearing voices itself, that the experiences of voice hearers is another instance of the interpenetration of empirical and fictional realities, i.e., the inception of a new world.

There is another stunning example of this marginal practice, this time to be found in the literary output of a noted science-fiction writer, Philip K. Dick.

Dick's version of the same marginal practice that Jung inaugurated can usefully be approached by a study of his book, *Valis*, in conjunction with his posthumously published *Exegesis* (*The Exegesis of Phillip K. Dick*) which is a partial collection of Dick's "mad" writings as he tried to come to grips with a revelation he had in 1974: "a sudden, discorporating slippage into vast and total knowledge that he would spend the rest of his life explicating, or exegeting."[54] [55] [56]

The posthumous publication of some of these texts highlights Dick's long and arduous attempt to understand what exactly was happening to him, in a similar manner to C. G. Jung's efforts, as recorded in *The Red Book*. I can choose any page at random to get a feel for sheer movement taking place, on-rushing fervour, a furore, gathering rapids, as punctuation breaks down, or ceases really to matter, as an onrushing life begins to prevail. It's like navigating a maelstrom at times, with little islands emerging only to be swept away again. The structure of that book is described as "a freewheeling voice that ranges through personal confession, esoteric scholarship, dream accounts, and fictional figures . . . one of the most improbable and mind-altering manuscripts ever brought to light."[57]

This kind of writing cannot be categorized because it is expressive of a breakdown of fundamental categories such as "inner" and "outer" and linear past, present, and future, those very categories that constitute the background of our stabilized modern structure of consciousness with its correlative empirical world.

One of the other significant category breakdowns relevant to Dick's writing is that of the pair of opposites: doing and reflection. Within our modern structure of consciousness we consider these a pair of opposites. We can do something in life or reflect on something in life but not both at the same time.[58]

In the kind of writing that Dick and Jung did, it seems that both happen simultaneously or something else happens that subsumes both within itself. I call this "happening" participation, after Owen Barfield.[59] Dick participates with the mind in its breakdown and writes it as he participates with it, as Jung apparently did. Thus, participation can be sharply distinguished from automatic writing where the writer's consciousness plays no part. It is also different from having an experience and subsequently writing about that experience from memory. The writing that emerges from this participatory process therefore is a form, or better, a forming (it's probably too early to call it a genre) that embodies such category breakdowns (inner/outer, past/present/future, action/reflection, etc.)

Such writing will appear crazy, as writers of this emerging marginal practice are forced to express mind-bending notions that are faithful to the phenomenon yet incoherent when subjected to the requirements of our stable modern form of consciousness.

A key methodological approach in producing this kind of "mad" writing is that the author takes seriously whatever phenomenon presents itself, in its own terms. The author must be able to remain "within" the phenomenon long enough so that it can teach her what it means in terms of its own logic, no matter how crazy it may sound when appraised from the categories of our current form of consciousness. The author is thus compelled to think self-presentational thoughts that defy ordinary rationality, as they think themselves out in her.

To take this line of argument a step further, we can ask what happens if, when the very categories that support our current form of consciousness break down, we stay immersed, participating in the chaos that logically follows, as Dick does. The process becomes mad and both *Exegesis* and *Valis* feel that way, from the perspective of our modern-day consciousness.

Valis and *Exegesis* are both accounts of the real process that a human being undergoes if she is pulled in to participation with the mind as it undergoes an epochal breakdown, so that all the categories that support modern consciousness (especially spatial and temporal categories) go under, taking the author with them, sometimes into insanity, but as we can see with Phillip K. Dick, also into sanity, the kind of sanity that our normal consciousness will judge as insane.

In just one small example that suggests strongly an incursion of fictional reality into empirical reality, Dick recounts:[60]

> The subject of this speech is a topic which has been discovered recently and which may not exist at all. It's a common theme in my writing that a dark-haired girl shows up at the door of the protagonist and tells him that his world is delusional, there is something false about it. Well, this did finally happen to me. I even knew that her hair would be black. I had an actual complete

sense of what she would look like and what she would say. She did appear. She was a total stranger and she did inform me of this fact: some of my fictional works were, in some literal sense, true.

This art form cannot only be deliberate, even though I said earlier that Jung willed his way into fictional reality. Giegerich shows convincingly that as a whole, the experience of *The Red Book* "was a deliberate technical undertaking", although "[t]here was certainly spontaneity within this experiment and for the experiencing subject."[61]

The Red Book does not simply represent an *avant garde* art movement with its conscious program. Throughout Jung's accounts of his psychic experiences, as recorded in *The Red Book*, as well as his autobiography, and other publications, he emphasizes the qualities of his experience as fictional reality interpenetrates with empirical reality. He insists that the encounters he has with imaginal figures are "spontaneous", "immediate", "autonomous", with a "compelling presence", "unintentional" etc.

In a similar way, Philip K. Dick engaged in deliberate experimentation (such as massive doses of vitamins, or amphetamines) during his eight-year long ordeal, within which, like Jung, he experienced many spontaneous happenings that convinced him of alternate realities as well.

This complex phenomenology points to an unheard-of "art form" in the making, one that "requires" a union of differences: empirical reality with its correlative (wilful, unitary) consciousness and fictional reality with its will as displayed in a plurality of consciousnesses:[62]

> Suppose nothing else were "given" as real except our world of desires and passions, and we could not get down, or up, to any other "reality" besides the reality

of our drives—for thinking is merely a relation of these drives to each other: is it not permitted to make the experiment and to ask the question whether this "given" would not be sufficient for also understanding on the basis of this kind of thing the so-called mechanistic (or "material") world? . . .

Apparently, for fictional reality to make an impression on such a consciousness that Nietzsche describes here, it must appear as a stronger will, one that subjects the wilful modern ego to *its* experiments. Only then can fictional reality initiate the modern ego into its, fictional reality's reality, i.e., having the same status as empirical reality, but remaining as fictional.

THE VIOLENT CHARACTER OF
THE NEW "ART FORM"

Since I still don't know enough about pain,
this terrible darkness makes me small.
If it's you, though—
press down hard on me, break in
that I may know the weight of your hand,
and you, the fullness of my cry.

Rilke

Jung's engagement with *The Red Book* continued for his entire life but the most intense period lasted about twenty years.[63] He later called this time his "confrontation with the unconscious"—and it was a time marked by violence:[64]

- I . . . decided I was menaced by a psychosis . . .
- An incessant stream of fantasies had been released . . .
- I stood helpless before an alien world . . .
- I was living in a constant state of tension . . . I felt as if gigantic blocks of stone were tumbling down upon me . . .
- One thunderstorm followed another. My enduring these storms was a question of brute strength. Others have been shattered by them . . .
- I was frequently so wrought up that I had to do certain yoga exercises to hold my emotions in check . . .
- In order to grasp the fantasies . . . I knew I had to let myself plummet down into them, as it were. I felt not only violent resistance to this, but a distinct fear . . .
- I had the following dream [of killing Siegfried]. When I awoke from the dream . . . a voice within me said, "You must understand the dream and must do so at once! . . . If you do not understand the dream you must shoot yourself!" In the drawer of my night table lay a loaded revolver . . .
- I hit upon this stream of lava, and the heat of its fires reshaped my life . . .

These are not accounts of violent dreams that Jung had. They are accounts of his waking life as he encountered fictional reality, or suffered the after-shocks. But he wasn't merely a victim of an unwanted attack, either. As he says in the same chapter:

It was my purpose to know what was going on within myself, I would do these [yoga] exercises only until I had calmed myself enough to resume my work with the unconscious. As soon as I had the feeling that I was myself again, I abandoned this restraint upon the emotions and allowed the images and inner voices to speak afresh.

In 1934, Jung presented a seminar on Nietzsche's *Thus Spake Zarathustra*.[65] This appears to be shortly after he emerged from his "confrontation with the unconscious". With a little more distance from his wrenching experiences, he now seemed able to begin the task of giving form to his ordeal. In the seminars, Jung turns to the motif of suspension that appears in Nietzsche's book at the point where Zarathustra "buries the corpse in a hollow tree."[66] Jung's interpretation of this motif clearly is also a hermeneutic exposition of his own ordeal (and perhaps the first). Yet it is so difficult to understand that, to date, no one has subsequently explored or developed this thought any further in terms of the material of *The Red Book*.

Perhaps the most significant reason that Jung's discussion of "suspension" is so difficult to grasp is that it is almost impossible to language. Jung's years-long ordeal, as recorded in *The Red Book* was also a sustained experience of suspension, as he encountered purely fictional figures. If the images of fictional reality are first and foremost figures of speech, then we are approaching a profound mystery when we undergo experiences with them, as Jung did:[67]

> For the great mystery . . . is this: the appearance of a speaking figure, the very embodiment as it were in human-divine form of clear, articulated, play-related and therefore enchanting, language—its appearance in that deep primordial darkness where one expects only animal muteness, wordless silence, or cries of pleasure and pain.

In my view Jung's ordeal was first and foremost an undergoing of such an experience with language, in the sense that Heidegger means:[68]

> To undergo an experience with something [here language] means that this something, which we reach

> along the way in order to attain it, itself pertains to us,
> meets and makes its appeal to us, in that it transforms
> us into itself . . . We speak and speak about language.
> What we speak of, language, is always ahead of us. Our
> speaking merely follows language constantly. Thus we
> are continually lagging behind . . . Accordingly, when
> we speak of language we remain entangled in a speaking
> that is persistently inadequate.

Thus, when Jung attempts to interpret the motif of suspension in *Thus Spake Zarathustra*, springing from the soil of his own suspension, he is forced to draw amplificatory material from the wide resource of his own scholarly background. For example he speaks of suspension as:[69]

- an aspect of crucifixion;
- the unconscious aspect of transfiguration;
- transformation being the fate of the body;
- transfiguration being the fate of the subtle body;
- preceding birth or creation;
- incubation of the subtle body;
- producing superior knowledge (like Odin's suspension and the art of writing);
- identification of the creator with what he is going to bring forth (see Heidegger quote above);
- torment in order to incarnate the unconscious contents;
- giving body to thoughts through "artistic" production;
- suspended ideas that express themselves as bodily symptoms;
- unconscious contents that "eat the sacrificed body" so that they can incarnate;
- ideas that take possession of the body;
- an initiatory process of "denying the body", inflicting terrible suffering so that a body can be produced in the mind.

In reading the transcript of Jung's seminar, including the section on the motif of suspension, I am struck by the sheer force and flow of his extemporaneous language which seems to be a fountain or spring, flowing over with images drawn from scholarship but, at the same time, revivified by new meaning, as Jung appropriated (in the sense of hermeneutics) Nietzsche's work to his efforts of giving voice to his own violent ordeal of suspension.

For all Jung's efforts here in the Seminars and subsequently throughout his life, this process of suspension that characterized his ordeal as recorded in *The Red Book* remains a profound mystery and has received little attention by subsequent commentators. As I said earlier, Hillman and Shamdasani take another view: that Jung is writing in a way that:[70]

> evokes the poetic basis of mind with a rhetoric that does not disabuse the psyche of its natural way of talking, and that requires a sensitivity to the words so that they imply, they suggest, it's a sensitivity to the language.

This interpretation of *The Red Book* simply appropriates Jung's work to Hillman's program (Archetypal Psychology) and completely ignores the phenomenology of the ordeal which involved the empirical Jung as he encountered fictional reality in a condition of suspension. One can, after all, learn the practice of "seeing through" to the archetypal background of modern phenomena, without in the least becoming "suspended".

Wolfgang Giegerich certainly acknowledges the phenomenon of torture in *The Red Book* and goes to considerable lengths in analysing it as a soul phenomenon.[71] [72] His project is to show how Jung's notion of the unconscious as a positivized factual reality within the empirical man was "installed".[73]

> A prolonged step-by-step process of sinking the form of
> thought into the form of the individual's . . . existential
> experience "in the flesh."

This is a process which to a large extent has the nature of a painful
suffering (up to the point of near-madness) and is accordingly
experienced as "cruel," a very frequent word in *The Red Book*.
The torment was absolutely necessary to really, and absolutely
convincingly, install the new arena in factual, bodily felt existence,
in man as mere Dasein.

There can be no doubt that Jung later reified his ordeal into a
dogma concerning the nature of god and his psychology of the
unconscious:[74] [75] [76]

- I cannot conceive of any religious belief that is less
  than a violation of my ego-consciousness;
- The I suffers violence from the Self;
- God is an apt name given to all overpowering
  emotions in my own psychic system, subduing my
  conscious will and usurping control over myself;
- This is the name by which I designate all things
  which cross my wilful path violently and recklessly,
  all things which upset my subjective views, plans,
  and intentions and change the course of my life for
  better or worse.

Giegerich's project is to valorise the unity of thinking and thought,
fiction and truth. He concludes that Jung tears fantasy (the form of
fantasy) and truth apart as two opposite realities, that Jung wants to
identify truth with factual existence, as if it [truth] were a piece of
nature: 'An elephant is true because it exists'. [77] [78]

Giegerich's analysis here of the ontological "purpose" of Jung's
ordeal is consistent with his (Giegerich's) view of art which he
explicates by reference to Dante's *Divine Comedy*:[79]

The fantasy content [of the Comedy] was relentlessly let go of and in this way allowed to find its own center of gravity and source of authority solely within itself as imaginal or fantastic . . .

Art-making requires taking a plunge. The fantasy (the idea, the image) is precisely allowed to be "nothing but" fantasy . . . . And only through this going under of the artist's subjectivity into the fantasy as self-sufficient and an end in itself does the art-work also obtain true objectivity . . . .

Art-making is the relentless working off of the duality of subject (author) versus object, experience (Content) versus representation (form), origin or cause versus result, in favor of the singularity of the work of art that has everything it needs within itself. Dante's work speaks for itself . . . [I]t is not a report about inner experiences from "the unconscious," not his "individuation process" . . .

It's critical for my discussion at this point to understand that Giegerich is basing his analysis of *The Red Book* on this, his view, of what constitutes art! Thus his analysis is a vehicle for appropriating (hermeneutically) the text of *The Red Book* to his project, just as Hillman did. Giegerich wants to establish psychology as a true discipline of interiority and to do so he has spent a life-time re-working (deepening) Jung's essential concepts into a more adequate form that resolves the neurotic structure of psychology that Jung constructed out of his (Jung's) own interpretation of his ordeal.[80][81]

Giegerich's conception of art and art-making is informed by the past and by the ontological structure which has been hardening over centuries: the distinction and then disjunction between (what has now become empirical reality or Heidegger's Dasein) and fictional reality (the unreal). There can, however, be no doubt today that art forms no longer carry the same ontological weight as empirical reality, no matter how much we may be gripped by the "truth" of the *Comedy* etc., as Giegerich clearly is.

I came across a compelling example of this fact during a visit to an art museum recently. The central piece on exhibit was a picture by Holman Hunt entitled: *The Light of the World*.

Here is an image of the awe inspiring guest knocking portentously on our door. Next to the picture was a reporter's account of what happened in 1906, when the painting was first shown in Sydney. The following report is drawn from the Daily Telegraph, 1906:

> Before 2 o'clock yesterday afternoon, almost 2000 people were waiting for the doors of the art gallery to open, and before the doors were closed again at 5 0'clock, 23080 people had passed through the turnstiles to see Holman Hunt's picture, "The Light of the World."

> The crowd was enormous. Once or twice, when the doors were closed against any further invasion of the building until those inside passed out, thousands gathered in solid mass against the entrance door and waited for admittance. Then when the doors were opened there was an extraordinary struggle. Women had their hats broken, blouses deranged, blouse belts and sashes torn or broken. Men pushed forward from the back, and men pushed backward from the front. Out of the struggling came the crying of terrified children Here two mites sobbed a request to be put through a window so they might speed home from a hitherto unknown battle of humans; there two policemen carried to a corner the stiffened figure of a woman who had fainted. Clearing themselves from the contortions of the crowd, many women found out spaces, where they touched up the little damages that had befallen them—hats were straightened out, tousled hair made tidy, and dresses smoothed down—for all the world like an indignant number of hens preening feathers after unexpectedly half-drowned with a deluge of water.

> Then came the closing of the doors again, with the police perspiring like firemen in a stokehold in their efforts to cut off the crown that was pouring in. Dozens

of younger men clambered up and jumped through open windows. It was a maddened race of modern pilgrims to a new shrine—a riot of curiosity.

Up stairs to the big picture the crowd went in endless clattering procession—old men, young men, boys, women of all ages, and little children holding each other's hands. In front of "the Light of the World" they stood and wondered if they had found what they had expected—wondered if they were pleased or disappointed. It was impossible to gauge the thoughts of the crowd—to understand what the picture said to the thousands of eyes that flung eagerly upwards to discover its possessions for their keeping, its rewards for their curiosity, its lessons for their remembrance.

Always the faces remained unchanged. One felt that the wave that had rushed itself through the doorways and gallery should here have had its climax of enthusiasm at the foot of the picture, but it was not there. Almost within a yard of the great work a girl busied herself in re-arranging a feather in her companion's hat; and two little lads, bent half over the railing by the weight of the crowd, discussed vehemently business connected with the sale and purchase of a pair of pigeons. In a dozen different places in the crowd, one heard the men who talked of the aims of art; the man who praises or blames the technique of the picture; and the girl who described the picture as "Nice!"

A few minutes in front of the picture sufficed most of those who came, and then they wandered around the galleries. Never before did art receive so much attention in Sydney.

Now in 2013, one hundred years on, what can we make of this extraordinary event? Clearly the Sydney art lovers were turning to the Coming Guest with anticipation, love, longing, and enthusiasm, at first anyway! Then it all went wrong! As we saw, the longing was quickly quenched in the moment that one might expect fulfilment. The reason for this I propose is that, for the people of Sydney in 1906, as it is for us now even more, the outer positive reality of the painting occludes, rather than opens up to the soul factor that once animated the picture (the factor that transforms the blobs of paint into art). While the anticipation of the coming guest opened hearts, and quelled noisy minds, the fact of the coming guest's arrival i.e., as a painting that was only experienced in its positivity in accord with our historical times, completely quelled all anticipations much like a product extinguishes the desire that is aroused by advertising.

I think it is a mistake to only judge *The Red Book* in terms of a concept of art that no longer obtains today. Jung's much noted passage in which he programmatically claims that "no, it is not art" reveals that something is at stake for him.[82] What is at stake is a new definition of art! I believe this new definition of art and artist is along the lines stated by Rosenberg:[83]

> [A]rt consists of one-person creeds, one-psyche cultures. Its direction is toward a society in which the experiences of each will be the ground of a unique, inimitable form—in short, a society in which everyone will be an artist. Art in our time can have no other social aim—an aim dreamed of by modern poets, from Lautreamont to Whitman, Joyce and the Surrealists, and which is embodied the essence of the continuing revolt against domination by tradition.

The violence that Jung experienced is necessary to this new art form. Empirical Reality's sole claim on reality is challenged by the unreal: fictional reality. Empirical reality insists on its supremacy and this obdurateness can only be challenged (or threatened) by another reality that can meet it on its own terms. Jung was faced with a reality that was every bit as real as empirical reality—as convincing as Johnson's rock, while at the same time, irreducible to empirical reality. Fictional reality penetrates empirical reality in a contest of wills. It is the isolated monad of the empiricist that is violated. The penetration involves the empirically real body in a way that is yet to be languaged. As I said, Jung drew from a vast reservoir of amplificatory material to try to give form to his experience. And as Wolfgang Giegerich has shown he carved out a psychology based on his confused or prejudiced conceptions of what had happened to him. Giegerich has subsequently single-handedly developed an internally consistent theory and practice of depth psychology (Psychology as a Discipline of Interiority) from within the great and confused theoretical work of the thinker Jung.

What remains is to find adequate language that can give form to the new art and the new "artist". It is clear to me that this language must arise as Ereignis, an inception, from the "pre-world": the world-disclosing aspect of language that Heidegger is concerned with:[84]

> What is unspoken is not merely something that is not yet shown, what has not yet reached its appearance. That which must remain wholly unspoken is held back in the unsaid, abides in concealment s unshowable, is mystery. That which is spoken to us speaks as dictum in the sense of something imparted, something whose speaking does not even require to be sounded . . . . The essential being of language is saying as showing.

TOWARDS A NEW WORLD-DISCLOSING LANGUAGE

[O]ur freedom to disclose new worlds is our special human freedom. [T]his freedom implies that there is no fixed pre-existent set of possible worlds. Each world exists only once it is disclosed . . . . If being world-disclosers is our nature, that would explain why we feel a special joy when we are opening new worlds even on a more local scale than the transformations brought about by Jesus or Descartes.

Hubert Dreyfus

John C. Woodcock

The Red Book is an inaugural effort of the "artist" Jung to disclose a new world by saying it. The years he engaged with fictional reality became his marginal practice which may contribute to the articulation of a new world in a work of art or cultural practice. Although he deviated from this "artistic" task into the conscious formulation of his depth psychology, he never lost sight of it, if we can judge from his continuing work on *The Red Book* and its publication over his life-time.

The task of "saying" this new world into being is daunting to say the least. I have already indicated the difficulties involved when two very sympathetic analysts of *The Red Book*, Hillman and Shamdasani, wrestle with the phenomenology of Jung's experiences. For example, they ask, did Jung write as he encountered fictional reality or did he record after the fact, through memory? In framing the issue this way they are opening up a distinction between participation and reflection. This distinction has a long history within philosophical inquiry but may be put simply as the difference between being and reflection and their increasing separation over millennia. As reflecting consciousness gained ascendancy, from "Descartes" on, our culture has become increasingly removed from Being and philosophy turned its attention more and more to theories that sprung from reflective consciousness to ask questions about Being.[85]

It seems to me that we are in a time where this disjunction between reflection and being is breaking down and "artists" such as Jung and, as we will see, Philip K. Dick, are pointing to this breakdown and the emergence of another way altogether. Thus, what Jung is "saying" to us through *The Red Book* is a language in which being and reflection are united in some new way that, as yet, we have no word for.[86] We have to be taught by the phenomenon. I have already given the examples of Jung's "eating the liver of a little girl", and that of the *Leontocephalus* (the lion-head), in which Jung is reporting an experience of interpenetration with fictional reality which involves this union of participation and reflection. In his own words:[87]

> You cannot get conscious [i.e., reflection—my insert] of these unconscious facts without giving yourself to them [i.e., participation—my insert]. If you can overcome your fear of the unconscious and let yourself down, then these facts take on a life of their own. You can be gripped by these ideas so that you really go mad, or nearly so. These images have so much reality that they recommend themselves, and so much extraordinary meaning that one is caught.

It seems clear to me from Jung's accounts of his and his subsequent commentary, that he is already struggling with language: "you cannot get conscious of these unconscious facts without giving yourself over to them". This is an initial, clumsy formulation, based on his later notion of the unconscious, of a phenomenon that utterly defies attempts to understand it in terms of categories of experience that it has left behind.

But Jung is not alone with the task of "saying" the new world. Owen Barfield gives us the concept of philosophical double-vision which points us to the kind of experience that Jung and Dick endured—the interpenetration of empirical reality and fictional reality.[88]

> There is a certain kind of nocturnal dream, in which we dream with one part of ourselves, and yet at the same time we know with another part that we are dreaming. The dream continues, and is a real dream (that is, it is not a waking reverie). And yet we know that we are dreaming; we are there outside the dream, as well as being there within it. I think we may let ourselves be instructed by such dreams in the nature of true vision.

It is from within such experiences that language will appear that conveys the unity of the difference between being and reflection and which inaugurates a new world.[89]

Philip K. Dick also underwent a sustained (eight years) and violent experience of language that almost drove him mad, while, at the same time, disclosing a world that is very similar to Jung's:[90]

> The process of its [Exegesis] production was frantic, obsessive, and it may be fair to say, involuntary. The creation of Exegesis was an act of human survival in the face of a life-altering crisis both intellectual and emotional: the crisis of revelation . . . that came to the person of Philip K. Dick in February and March of 1974 and subsequently demanded, for the remainder of Dick's days on earth, to be understood . . . not for the sake of his own psyche, nor for the cause of the salvation of humankind, but precisely because those two concerns seemed to him to be one and the same.

The phenomenology of Dick's ordeal is remarkably similar to Jung's as is his response to the phenomenon: to understand the revelatory fictional material that was "breaking in on him". In fact there is one biography of Dick that is called Divine Invasions![91] Both men experienced violent breakdown in the usual categories of inner/outer, real/fiction, body/spirit, for example, and they both tried to find a form in which to articulate their experiences.

There is a well-known widely defined form of literature called Magical Realism in which the process which Jung and Dick went through in actuality is explored fictionally. Magical Realism explores the impact fictional reality has on ordinary reality. Jorge Luis Borges, a major proponent of this genre, offers a remarkable fictional account of the phenomenon of fictional reality penetrating into empirical reality with his short story, "Tlön, Uqbar, Orbis, Tertuis".[92] In this story, a Volume of a mysterious encyclopaedia is discovered. Through a series of accidents, or chance connections, the narrator discovers that a purely fictional world exists (Tlön) and the encyclopaedia is describing its culture, languages, etc. The story proceeds with a deeper description and involvement with that world, through reading the encyclopaedia, and "events became more intense". This purely fictional reality begins to slowly bleed into empirical reality! Small items that had hitherto belonged only to Tlön, now show up *as such* in empirical reality (the world of the narrator).

Wikipedia calls this "magical" event one of the major themes which illustrate the principle that "ideas ultimately manifest themselves in the physical world and the story is generally viewed as a parabolic discussion of Berkeleian idealism . . ."[93]

I believe this interpretation entirely misses the point of Magical Realism. The notion that ideas manifest in empirical reality is of course a version of idealism—ideas manifest as art, cultural works, good deeds, etc. This is not news. Borges is making another, more startling, claim. He writes in this short story:

> In 1942 events became more intense . . . . It happened in an apartment . . . Princess Faucigny Lucinge had received her silverware . . . delicate immobile objects emerged . . . . Amongst them—a compass vibrated mysteriously. The princess did not recognize it. Its blue needle longed from magnetic north; its metal case was concave in shape; the letters around its edge corresponded to one of the alphabets of Tlön. Such was the first intrusion into the world of reality.

A purely fictional item had spontaneously penetrated into empirical reality *as that very fictional item!*

In this way Borges is exploring, in literature, a phenomenon that as yet has no adequate formulation. But it does have its "mouthpieces", among them Jorge Luis Borges!

C. S. Lewis explores the same phenomenon, in reference to the books of Charles Williams, as the effect of the "marvelous" invading the ordinary: [94]

> [In Williams' novels]: We meet, on the one hand, very ordinary modern people who talk the slang of our own day and who live in the suburbs. On the other hand we also meet the supernatural—ghosts, magicians, and archetypal beasts. The first thing to grasp is that this not a mixture of two literary kinds. That's what some readers suspect and resent. They acknowledge on the one hand straight fiction: the classical novel, as we know it from Fielding to Goldsworthy. They acknowledge on the other the pure fantasy which creates a world of its own cut off in a kind of ringed fence, from reality—books like Wind in the Willows . . . and they complain that Williams is asking them to skip to and fro from one to the other in the same work. But Williams is really writing a third kind of book which belongs to neither class and has a different value from either. He is writing that sort of book in which we begin by saying, "Let us suppose that this everyday world were at some one point invaded by the marvelous".

Williams' books brilliantly describe the process of manifestation as purely fictional realities "invade" empirical reality:[95]

> She was where he had left her, but a dreadful change was coming over her. Her body was writhing into curves and knots where she lay, as if cramps convulsed her. Her mouth was open, but she could not scream; her hands were clutching at her twisted throat. In her wide eyes there was now no malice, only an agony, and gradually

all her body and head were drawn up backwards from the floor by an invisible force, so that from the hips she remained rigidly upright and her legs lay stretched straight out behind her upon the ground, as if a serpent in human shape raised itself before him . . .

The face rounded out till it was perfectly smooth, with no hollows or depressions, and from her nostrils and her mouth something was thrusting out. In and out of her neck and hands an—other skin was forming, over or under her own—he could not distinguish which, but growing through it, here a coating, there an underveiling. Another and an inhuman tongue was flicking out over a human face . . .

Although this is a fictional rendering of the interpenetration of fictional reality with empirical reality, we can see an immediate similarity with Jung's *actual* experience of the *Leontocephalus*. Throughout his works, Williams links the quality of violence with purity of desire. I can verify this intuition through my own experiences of such incursions, where I write:[96]

At the peak of my ecstasies, I met a being who I called my beloved Star Sister. She came to me while I was fully awake, alone in my bed. I could get out of bed and see quite clearly with my outer vision that I was alone yet I also saw, felt, and touched her there beside me, as real as my knowledge that I was alone. Both realities were interpenetrating each other. It was then that I experienced myself as being loved by another, totally as an object of divine desire. Here I learned that the human body is able to receive an influx of love from the Beyond. It is the organ of the heart that is the door and it is the self-imposed limitations of the ego that close the door. I felt fearful that I could not contain it and was told again and again by my divine lover that I could,

> that I needed only to open up completely, right to the
> level of the cells of my body. I discovered that I could
> do this and in that condition of complete surrender I
> received the poetry that came to me.

Borges and Williams, along with other artists belonging to the genre of Magical Realism, are exploring the strange interpenetration of fictional reality with empirical reality *fictionally*. That is to say, there is no hint that the author himself has experienced such "events". In the case of C. G. Jung and Philip K. Dick, then, we seem to have evidence that what Magical Realism is exploring fictionally, became a reality for these two authors! They are reporting to us what really happens when fictional reality bursts into empirical reality.

As fictional reality penetrates into empirical reality, the quality of violence reflects the psychological preparedness of the empirical personality (Williams' "purity of desire"). For Jung, it seems to have been a quality of a "battle of wills"; Dick's process has been likened to mania, or even neurological damage due to amphetamine abuse.[97] In my own case my own psychology was characterized by equal proportions of terror and joy and the violence I suffered mirrored this conflict in its manifestations. Underlying these individual variations is an Ereignis: an incursion, an inception, as fictional reality brings its reality home to modern consciousness—a consciousness that privileges empirical reality and has downgraded any other reality to unreality.

In my book, *Overcoming Solidity: World Crisis and the New Nature*, I present just one example of the extreme level of violence that can occur as fictional reality breaks into empirical reality, when the personality is completely unprepared for, and ignorant of, fictional reality as a *reality*.[98] In other words, since modern consciousness is completely occluded, with its sole focus on the surface of things, fictional reality must appear as equally obdurate: an irresistible force meets an immovable object—a train wreck in the making![99]

WHAT KIND OF WORLD?

[Ereignis] means, roughly, a kind of experience in which I find myself intimately involved, as opposed to an experience in which I am nothing but an objective viewer. [I]t means, roughly, the possible happening in which a new dwelling may be founded—a place and age in which a people could cultivate significance.

Heidegger suggests that only a non-theoretical thinking can do justice to Ereignis. Such thinking cannot simply present a disengaged report on Ereignis, but must take part in it and flow from it.

Richard Polt

Fictional reality wants to gain the same status as empirical reality, by penetrating empirical reality.[100] This is what "artists" in their marginal practice, such as Jung and Dick, are showing us. How can it do this *as* fictional reality? What would that look like? It would have to become as real as empirical reality, yet distinct; maintaining its logical status as fictional reality and yet being a real world, a new house or dwelling for us. We would have to consider the possibility of embodied story, manifest word, and sensual language. What could this mean today?

Robert Graves, the great 20th. C. muse-poet and scholar, understood the intimate, undivided relationship between language and reality. He could thus say:[101]

> The function of poetry is religious invocation of the Muse, its use is the experience of mixed exaltation and horror her presence excites . . . . as a warning to man that he must keep in harmony with the family of creatures among which he was born . . . it is now a reminder that he has disregarded the warning and turned the house upside down . . . and brought ruin on himself and his family.

We need to very clear here about what Graves is saying in regards to the function of poetry: "the religious invocation" of the Muse. He is not talking about poetry or words that intend to induce a "thrill" in the audience, the way Sentimental or Gothic genres do. These only came into existence as the interiority or inwardness of nature withdrew and settled in us, so that, like children, we had a certain amount of control over the image and wanted to play with that power. We could use images, the more fantastic the better, to evoke shock or excitement in us and we eagerly sought such experiences, since we had become painfully aware of the loss of Meaning in nature.[102]

"Invoking the Muse" is the mantic utterance of language. There is power in that language for good or ill. The Muse is the interiority of that language (or world) whose presence becomes visible, palpable, sensual, there! There is no private thought of "me" being thrilled. There is only the Muse and the mood that belongs to her and her world. The Muse poet evokes a world and Graves tells us the moods that belong to that world: exaltation, horror, and warning.

I do not agree with Graves that we humans have merely disregarded her warnings. There is the question of worlds coming and going, as Heidegger reminds us. Her world has gone so She cannot be invoked anymore. Language and world have transformed. We live in our technological civilization with its own invocatory language.[103]

Yet we do have faint echoes of Her world still alive in our language. How is it, for example, that a single well-placed word can cause blood (the autonomic system) to rush to the "victim's" face in a flush of embarrassment? Our positivist world cannot hope to account for this mantic use of language. We also know of the problem of "dissing" in some subcultures (no respect) where retaliatory violence can be evoked.

Graves reminds us of the time of the great Irish and Welsh poets:[104]

> The Irish and Welsh distinguished carefully between poets and satirists: the poet's task was creative or curative, that of the satirist was destructive or noxious. An Irish poet could compose an aer, or satire, which would blight crops, dry up milk, raise blotches on his victim's face and ruin his character forever.

These powers were only possible when the lived-world was the language of the goddess.

Leo Tolstoy is a Celtic scholar who brings the Celtic world alive for us via the "historical novel". He describes how the Ollave or Welsh master-poet shifts into the state of mind from which his poetry may burst forth:[105]

> [I]t was the turn of Taliesin, chief of bards, to sing before the company. It was easy to see from his foaming lips and shining brow that the awen [muse] was upon him . . . . [H]e rose to resume that which can never perish: immortal song, for which the poet's utterance is but the mouthpiece of the godhead, the outpouring of the Cauldron of Poesy . . . . We were no longer within Brochfael's great hall . . . but flew with winged thoughts wherever Taliesin's honeyed words bore us.

As I have shown elsewhere, this "time" is a status of consciousness-world in which the present dichotomy between empirical reality and fictional reality had not yet occurred.[106] Words still had the power to transport us into what was then the really real. This reality was always close at hand and ordinary reality dissolved readily into it. Tolstoy devotes entire chapters to the phenomenon of giving way to this deeper reality that is "always there".[107]

Jung and Dick's experiences give us the hint that, today, the direction is reversed. Empirical reality simply cannot "give way" to the deeper reality. Empirical reality is that reality that is surface only. The deeper reality, now downgraded to fictional reality, is bursting forth and penetrating empirical reality with varying degrees of violence, as I have said. Thus, the marginal practice that explores this process of the interpenetration of empirical reality and fictional reality will be a different "artistic" form from that of Taliesin, for example. We will not be transported by the mantic use of language into a deeper reality that lies behind and around ordinary reality.

The quality of "story" will be quite different!

We are hearing the beginnings of such storying, for example, in UFO reports of abduction. One of the most compelling aspects of these accounts is the abductees' insistence that it really happened, that the abduction is concretely real—this in the face of not a shred of empirical evidence! The "victims" will not entertain the notion that they dreamed it, or hallucinated. They universally describe themselves as not inclined to give way to fancy and not particularly psychological in their outlook. They are, in fact, describing themselves in terms of Heidegger's Dasein: what you see is what you get. Nothing below the surface here! I just do what everyone does in this life, etc. This description belongs to the consciousness correlative to empirical reality today.

Similarly, accounts given by many Voice Hearers (see Chapter: *Interpenetration of Realities*, above) show the same phenomenology: an experience of a really real voice that breaks into empirical reality and is so often mistaken for such. Not only voices, but other sensually real appearances occur as well. One voice hearer told me of her experiences at night in which a man would regularly enter her bed and touch her all over. She "could feel everything"! I could immediately relate to her story though my own encounter with my "Star Sister" (see Chapter: *Interpenetration of Realities*, above) as well as other similar experiences such as this one:[108]

> I am in bed and I am dreaming of a woman who is inside of me skin to skin. She is beginning to separate from me and is kissing me from the inside, making love to me. I am aroused but also scared too. It feels uncanny to have someone in my skin, sharing my body. I begin turning to see her. I want to see her but she resists me. It's like one body moving to two separate wills. I get scared but I manage to turn around expecting to see a witch. I see a young woman. I look into her eyes deeply and I see the universe of stars. I keep thinking of the Knights Templar. I don't think she wants me to look at her. I feel possessed. I am aware that I am dreaming. She

comes out of my skin again and holds me down. It's like she is a little behind me. I can physically feel her arms and body. I turn around again and our mouths meet. Hers is like honey. She resists at first but her moistures are flowing. I touch her and we begin to make love. I feel both of us as we move together. She is distinguishable from me yet she came out of me.

Tolstoy's description of Taliesin's poesis does give us clue for developing the new art form. He says that Taliesin is a "mouthpiece for the godhead". Jung also invokes this image in his famous letter to Herbert Read:[109]

We have simply got to listen to what the psyche spontaneously says to us . . . . It is the great dream which has always spoken through the artist as mouthpiece.

Being a mouthpiece for the interpenetration of realities would therefore involve becoming a vehicle for the interpenetration to take place and speak itself into existence, through the mouthpiece. As Jung says further on in the same letter to Read:

If the artist of today could only see what the psyche is spontaneously producing and what he, as a consciousness, is inventing, he would notice that the dream f.i. or the object is pronouncing (through his psyche) a reality from which he will never escape, because nobody will ever transcend the structure of the psyche.

Our time is the time of empiricism which thinks of itself as the only reality. It seems, then, that the objective psyche, or fictional reality, is, at this time, pressing forward into empirical reality, gaining a body, as it were, so that its reality, equal to empirical reality, is pronounced in a convincing manner. This requires an "embodied language". I use the quotes to suggest that I do not mean merely the use of words, particularly the way words are used today, purely as instruments of communication in a subject-object world. As fictional reality begins to penetrate into empirical reality, the "artist" in this marginal practice will learn how to "say" it. This saying must at the same time be a doing, in order that fictional reality has the same "reality status" as empirical reality. The very doing of the artist's life will therefore be an unfolding of fictional reality, or story, consciously so. This new world will thus be disclosed in the deepening involvement of the artist in its origination.

This artistic method is quite different from what James Hillman offers through his Archetypal Psychology. His book, *Healing Fiction*, demonstrates how our personal history may be "seen through" to its archetypal image, dissolving the literalisms that constitute empirical reality.[110] In other words, empirical reality may be seen as a special kind of fictional reality—one in which it "believes only in literalisms". This theoretical move in made on the ontological basis of the poetic mind. He then examines clinical practice (case notes, diagnoses, and other literalisms) from the perspective that they are all simply stories, or fictions.[111]

Hillman goes on to describe his method:[112]

> We have to see the inner necessity of historical events, out there, in the events themselves, where 'inner' [is] . . . the subjectivity in events and that attitude that interiorizes events, goes into them in search of psychological events.

Hillman wants affirm psychic reality as the within-ness of empirical reality by gaining a psychological perspective of empirical events; to find the soul or inwardness of empirical reality, by turning an event into an experience: "we can regard [literal] history from the viewpoint of soul."

To engage in this artistic practice involves moving "backwards and inwards", from the literal to the imaginal or soulful. With this practice we can (he claims) discover the soul or depth of what would otherwise be merely a literal historical narrative. Wolfgang Giegerich criticizes this thought of Hillman's by showing that "the things themselves" today in fact have no "inner" that can be searched out. This is because our reality is now empirical reality, surface only. What Hillman is proposing then is a kind of make-believe, an as-if![113] Giegerich criticizes any attempt to "return" to the world of the goddess or to former states of consciousness that once prevailed but have now been overcome (i.e. self-overcome by soul in its own historical transformations).

He instead "locates" soul for us today as the "within-ness" of our language and has developed a coherent methodology that he calls a true psychology of the soul.[114] He has, for example, opened up the soul of our entire technological civilization, showing the historical depths of Being, of which the language, and therefore world of our technological civilization, are simply the manifestation.[115]

This form of soul work opens us to the abysmal depths of our past, so that we can understand our present as a historical phenomenon, i.e., not an absolute given.

The marginal practice that I am focussed on here, although related in the sense that it, too, can later become subject to such depth analysis, is, in essence a creative act, i.e., oriented to the future. The "artist" who is involved in "making worlds" is in the practice of creating what will, for later students of depth psychology, become soul history.

How does this work, in practice? I could put in this way. Hillman and Giegerich gaze into, say, an historical text, and disclose its soul, its interiority, that gave rise to the phenomenon in the first place, e. g. our technological civilization, as I have said. They discover the underlying image or logical life.

The marginal practice that characterizes the "world-making" artist moves in the opposite direction. She begins with Ereignis, an inception, which *penetrates*. A resonant derivative image (hint of the unknown future) arises spontaneously in her psyche and she participates in that future's continuing incarnation into empirical reality through "artistic" enactment, where it may gain form (see Jung's description of "suspension" above). This process involves the artist's conscious participation in forming the future (what will later become soul history)—a new world.

Soul, or fictional reality, is already working its way into material life through us, or through our actions, unconsciously, as we simply go about our business today. As each new idea, thought or image breaks into consciousness, the impressed image excites our desires (for fame, money, or power) and we quickly help it into incarnation, on the basis of self-interest, resulting in the world we inhabit today.

We now seem to be in a position where we can make choices about what aspect of fictional reality comes into actuality. And as Charles Williams says, what we choose and what the outcome is, depends on our inner preparation (what he would call "purity of desire"). Our mostly unconscious choices are producing a world that is increasingly hostile to all life. Aspects of fictional reality are indeed breaking into empirical reality through us, shaped by our unconscious desires into grotesque forms of horror, as Picasso shows us (see Chapter: *Art and Our Way of Being*) and as Owen Barfield writes:[116]

> Imagination is not, as some poets have thought, simply synonymous with good. It may be either good or evil. As long as art remained primarily mimetic, the evil which imagination could do was limited by nature ... [b]ut ... when the fact of the directionally creator relation is beginning to break through into consciousness, both the good and evil latent in the working of imagination begin to appear unlimited .... we could very well move

forward into a chaotically empty or fantastically hideous world . . . .

We should remember this, when appraising the aberrations of the formally representational arts . . . in so far as they are genuine, they are genuine because the artist has in some way experienced the world he represents. And in so far as they are appreciated, they are appreciated by those who themselves are willing to make a move towards seeing the world in that way and, ultimately therefore, seeing that kind of world. We should remember this, when we see pictures of a dog with six legs emerging from a vegetable marrow or a woman with a motor-bicycle substituted for her left breast.

As a marginal practice, the way of the "artist" prepares the unknown future by turning towards fictional reality with love, and receptivity as a mouthpiece (Barfield's "directionally creator relation"). She can distinguish between the desire of fictional reality and her own personal desires so that she can participate in realizing the desire of fictional reality: to tell and to generate further telling as a path to actualizing the as-yet-unknown future.

THE MARGINAL PRACTICE:
some examples

Each of these examples originates in an inception. An aspect of fictional reality penetrates my empirical life and begins to act on me. My response is to act. I begin to enact the inception as it resonates in me, like a bell sounding. In this way fictional reality begins to embody in empirical reality. As action follows action, the image or thought becomes more realized as a world that I inhabit. The empirical events that follow are formed by my participation with the image or thought that was impressed in me by Ereignis. Thus we can begin to see how fictional reality reveals itself in empirical reality but *as* fictional. In this way a possible future becomes my future: a union of telos and contingency!

My entire doctoral program was formed this way. The "originating" image was that of the lighthouse and it began to work its way into my life, becoming a new world of involvement that I had not known before. The course, outcome, and subsequent post-doctoral career together configure the world of the lighthouse. Here is the story.[117]

LIGHTHOUSE AT THE END OF THE WORLD

In 1997, I entered a Ph.D. program. This step was based on highly unusual and improbable events that had accumulated around me, acting as a sort of funnel into the future. I had no money and all other options seemed closed to me. I was despairing of my life which had been stripped down to the bone in order that I might participate in the incarnation of certain ideas that penetrated my being through the unconscious. A friend gave me the admissions brochure three times over a month and finally I accepted it, wrote out an application, and paid with a credit card. I had no idea how I would finance the program and indeed how I would even pay to get to the colloquium or even to buy a book.[118]

I was accepted, although the school did send me to a psychologist who checked me out to see if I was stable enough to last the distance. I was proposing to research what I myself had undergone: an apocalypse. I proposed that the end of the world theme in literature and in recorded historical events (such as dreams) could be explored as a soul phenomenon that occurs as the transformation of the individual as much as that of the world.

The course of my program, and its eventual outcome was not planned by me in advance at all. It unfolded from a dream:

> I visit Anita and she tells me she is dying with cancer, a very tender, very sad moment. We go to a busy bookstore where she breaks down and tells me that she has never been able to read books because she has never been able to find a still place inside. She has a boy friend that becomes threatening at one point. I see a lighthouse at the end of a long narrow peninsula and I feel excited about it. We must go visit it, I say.

A few days after this dream as I browsed through an online bookstore, I was startled to find a book called *The Lighthouse at the End of the World* by Stephen Marlowe.[119] I immediately thought of my dream lighthouse at the end of a long peninsula. The synchronicity brought together lighthouses, books, and the end of the world. I remembered also that Anita was raised as a Seventh Day Adventist. This religious denomination bases its spiritual guidance on *Revelation* and is centrally concerned with apocalyptic wisdom.

I began to feel that "something" in my life was gathering momentum. I felt a hidden significance to these events and they produced a moral response in me. I felt I needed to become attuned to these images, to synchronize my movements somehow to these hints.

I went shopping for Christmas and noticed a model lighthouse staring at me. I bought it. I was presented with a Christmas gift of a lighthouse calendar and on the Internet I found a lighthouse at Sequim, quite near where I lived. To get there, visitors must travel to the end of a long sandy peninsula, as in my dream. After a movie one night soon after, a friend and I drove through the city and became lost. It was very late at night and we were running low on gas. I turned a dark corner in an area of town under the freeway and there in the middle of the familiar waterfront buildings was a life-size replica of a lighthouse, fully lit up, indeed a beacon in the dark night.

Soon after returning home, I consulted the *I Ching* and received the hexagram for *The Wanderer*. The last line said: "Maintain your integrity! It may become your lighthouse in the sea of the unknown."

Something was approaching me through these unusual events and I did not need any more hints to pay close attention. I eagerly awaited Marlowe's book that, in one image, combined all the hints that I had received: lighthouses, the end of the world, and books. But I was still quite unprepared for what came next. When I received the book I was immediately gripped by the synopsis on the fly-leaf which described the book as an exploration of the convergence of two realities. This is close to the language I was using to formulate the phenomenology of the end of the world. I was proposing that the experience of the end of the world in contemporary times is one in which the Cartesian paradigm, based on a principle of separation of realities is being transformed into a new paradigm, based on a principle of interpenetration of realities.

I was equally startled by the fact that the book was based on the life of Edgar Allen Poe.

Poe was a childhood hero of mine. I had his collection of *Tales of Terror* and read them eagerly over many years—*The Pit and the Pendulum*, *The Maelstrom*, and *The Fall of the House of Usher* being my favorites. Poe is unrivalled as an artist expressing the form of literature known as Gothic Romance. I also had rediscovered him more recently in connection with another dream that had announced to me: "Your life is a High Gothic novel!"[120]

My own life, the Gothic imagination with its focus on the end of civilization through the eruption of the powers of chaos or forces of irrationality, and my work on the phenomenon of the end of the world, were all now linked in my imagination with the life and work of Edgar Allan Poe to whom I had been magnetically drawn as a child.

There was more to come . . .

My research into Gothic literature intertwined with yet another thread involving the symbols of the peacock, its connection to the comet, its role in my own life, and the phenomenology of the end of the world.[121] I therefore became speechless when I opened Marlowe's book to page two and found the fictional Poe narrating his confusion about the (historically factual), missing five days of his life, just before he died:

> Where had I gone, those five days? And what done?
> And in whose company? I had been on binges before.
> Surely that was the sum and substance of it, a not very
> mysterious mystery. But then why, in hospital, in what
> little remained to me of afterwards, did I sometimes call
> myself Mr. Peacock?*

There was an asterisk at the end and so I looked down to the footnote on page 3 and read, "It cannot be said with any certainty whether or not Mr. Poe knew that the word for "peacock" in Old Norse is poe."

So now, two more threads in what seemed to be an increasingly complex fabric began to weave together. And yes, throughout Marlowe's book there is a major role given to comets and the end of the world! As I continued my examination of his book I found a chapter which opened with Poe heading out to a lighthouse on a desolate island. He is trying to finish a book that had eluded him. In fact a footnote told me that when the historical Poe had died, he had left fragments of a book that was called: *The Lighthouse at the End of the World*. This was a thrilling discovery for me and I began to feel a weird sense that my life and Poe's were intertwined in some way that involved Gothic romance, peacocks, comets, lighthouses and the end of the world. I read on:[122]

> His unstrung nerves were, of course, what had brought
> Edgar there, two hundred miles from the nearest
> land . . . . His unstrung nerves were why he had been
> unable to finish the most ambitious work he had ever
> undertaken, a novel, as yet untitled, about the end of
> the world. Although the last few chapters remained
> to be written, he had not set pen to paper for months.

In that time the insidious idea grew that, possibly, the story had no ending. Was it too apocalyptic? Or too far beyond his imaginative powers? It had come to obsess him, to consume his every thought, his every waking hour. He drank little, ate less. He avoided social contact, persuading himself that that was the real problem, that people insisted on bedeviling him with talk, talk and more talk, when he craved the silence to immerse himself in the ending of the work he could not finish. Soon he began to dream of a writer, rather like himself, who was obsessed by a story he was struggling—with what desperation Edgar well knew—to finish; a story about the end of the world. His dream-self, deciding that isolation was the answer, sought employment as a lighthouse keeper.

I could feel the relevance of Poe's anguish over writing and finishing his book as my own in trying to give voice to my ordeal that had lasted for nearly twenty years.[123] I now eagerly turned to the beginning of the book and began to read. The structure of the book expresses an increasing complex interpenetration of dream, waking life, the fictional Poe and the empirical (historical) Poe. It felt so much like the unfolding of my own life that I felt unnerved. Inner and outer, self and other, past present and future, were in such close proximity, so relativised and intertwined, that the book approached an experience of madness that I knew so well.

Marlowe portrays an uncanny interpenetration of realities that are normally kept apart, within a deeper context of an apocalypse brought about by a comet. As I read on I felt a frightening sense of dissolving structures just as Emerson describes it in *The Over-Soul*:[124]

> The things we now esteem fixed shall, one by one, detach themselves, like ripe fruit from our experience, and fall. The wind shall blow them none knows whither.

> The landscape, the figures, Boston, London, are facts as
> fugitive as any institution past, or any whiff of mist or
> smoke, and so is society, and so is the world. The soul
> looketh steadily forwards, creating a world before her,
> leaving worlds behind her. She has no dates, nor rites,
> nor persons, nor specialties, nor men. The soul knows
> only the soul; the web of events is the flowing robe in
> which she is clothed.

Marlowe's story shows a collapse of fixed structures based on opposites, leading to an apocalypse. He created a fictional Poe who intersected with the historical Poe as if to stress that fiction and empirical reality also can no longer be kept apart.

A lighthouse at the end of the world! "Maintain your integrity— it may become your lighthouse in the sea of the unknown." A lighthouse: a place at the edge of the known universe sending out a light into the blackness of the abyss; a place at the edge, bleak, desolate, lonely, barren and dangerous—where sanity itself is tested; integrity as a lighthouse—able to withstand the storms of an apocalypse and at the same time, being a beacon of light.

My friend has a book on the table. My eyes widen for it is called *House of Light*, a collection of poems by Mary Oliver.[125] I tell my friend my tale of lighthouses and, of course, she gives me the book as a gift. I open it at random and find the the Buddha's last instruction: "Make of yourself a light". Ahh! Yes! The *I Ching* had also instructed me, and what was that dream I had, so many years ago?

> I am sitting at a table. A huge wind begins to buffet
> me. I start shaking as it gets stronger. I reach out and
> grab my mani stone which is sitting at the centre of
> the table and begin to chant Om Mani Padme Hum—
> praise to the jewel at the heart of the lotus—as the
> wind reaches a crescendo. I hear in the back—ground

a group of Tibetan monks supporting me, chanting too. The stone, the chant—I hold together. The wind abates. I have survived. The wind had pervaded my body and leaves me now with the ambiguity of whether the wind was a subtle one or my body had become more subtle, more light-like. There had been an interpenetration of realities! I remembered how, in previous dreams I had simply been blown away like a leaf, by these storms.

Edgar Allen Poe died at the age of 40. He lived on the edge and was assailed by the storms of the abyss:[126]

> Waves broke like thunder against the lighthouse, which seemed—was it possible—to sway . . . White water surged from all sides, submerging the base of the tower. The lenses of the lamp, opaque with streaming water, stared sightlessly out at the raging sea. For forty-eight hours, except for the wind and the surf, a world outside the walls of the lighthouse ceased to exist. And then it was over . . . Edgar prowled the living quarters until dusk . . . In the clockworks room once more, Edgar swiftly wrote "The Lighthouse at the End of the World", and in the solitude resumed at last to write.

Having survived the storm, he prepares to send a shaft of light out into the growing darkness . . .

Several months later, near the autumnal equinox of the year (1998), it was late at night, and I packed the last of my possessions into the car. I had released my connections to Seattle and was about to journey across the plains of Montana and North Dakota in order to join my fiancée in Michigan, a State that I knew nothing about.

Floating easily at 80 mph on the thin ribbon of road that stretches across the prairies I was reminded of my solitary motor bike journey across Australia so many years ago (1979), just before my coming to the USA. That journey had been a prelude to an enormous leap into the abyss. I had left my beloved Anita behind in Sydney, the very same Anita whose image appeared in my dream. As soon as I had reached the USA, I began a spiritual ordeal that was to span 20 years.

I wondered if this move would carry similar consequences.

My journey was uneventful and free. I felt as though with each passing mile old skins were shedding off my back and that I was being newly born. The expanse of grassy plains of the Dakotas was slowly replaced by the farming fields and ponds of Minnesota until, in the early pre-dawn, the time of Sophia, I arrived at the gray morning border of Michigan. I decided to go to the rest stop that was there to welcome tourists.

As I pulled in to the parking area, I barely noticed the large shape emerging from the foggy darkness. I was tired and felt inclined to ignore the lighthouse that slowly appeared, towering over me. Perhaps I was also a bit habituated to yet another one arriving spontaneously into my experience. But then I was jolted into alertness: A lighthouse! What the hell is a lighthouse doing here at a tourist welcome centre, in Michigan of all places?! I got out of my car and moved quickly over to the lighthouse to read the plaque nearby. To my complete astonishment I learned that Michigan is the State of lighthouses—hundreds are preserved around its lakes and the State uses a lighthouse logo, so proud it is of these legacies.

Now I knew that my arrival in Michigan carried my destiny and that there was an interpenetration of realities at hand. My dream had steered me to this State of lighthouses where I was to learn how to be a lighthouse in a storm that lasted five more years, taking me once again to the edge of madness.

I completed my thesis in 1999 amidst chaos. I came close to drowning: bankruptcy, a house almost burned down, and then later, homelessness, after selling the house to repay debts and end a broken marriage. After struggling to survive, for several years after graduation, I returned to Australia in 2003 to marry Anita, the girl of my dreams, literally (see above). There was still more chaos to bear as we both worked hard to form what is fondly called today a blended family. Gradually the waters receded and we found firm ground. I started up a small private practice and I called it *Lighthouse Down Under*, also the name of my website. I wrote a small poem for its index page:

> storm raging
> stones hold
> ray of light
> stretching the night
> touching the horizon

Like the fictional Edgar Allen Poe (see quote above, with apologies to Marlowe):

> Waves broke like thunder against the lighthouse, which seemed—was it possible—to sway . . . White water surged from all sides, submerging the base of the tower . . . . For [five years], except for the wind and the surf, a world outside the walls of the lighthouse ceased to exist. And then it was over . . . [I] prowled the living quarters until dusk . . . In the clockworks room once more, [I] swiftly wrote "Lighthouse at the End of the World", and in the solitude resumed at last to write.

I have since written ten books and they all are attempts to say what the lighthouse, with its bright beam of light always "touching the horizon", brings to my attention.

๛

The history of my life between 1997 and 2003 is an enactment of an aspect of fictional reality that had penetrated empirical reality and began to disclose a new world—the world of the lighthouse, which I increasingly became involved in. The inception was oriented towards the future, making a future, and I was its instrument. It was not a future based on a plan or goal that I had. I followed its hints and "pulls" into the unknown future, creating it as I acted, or *en*acted the dream's hint. I did not know what the dream meant and I still don't, unless I say that it meant (as its telos) the world (or mode of living) of the lighthouse in which I still dwell from time to time. I credit Russell Lockhart as the pioneer within the depth psychological tradition who first articulated the process of making the future. He writes:[127]

> I believe the eros of enactment generates meaning through doing and the consequences of doing, not through ideas of doing or mere understanding of images. [my italics]

Referring to Jung's famous letter to Sir Herbert Read he shows where such doing leads:

> The "great Dream" [or as Jung also says, "the future and picture of the new world—my insert] is born from following, submitting to, humbling oneself and one's ego to the hint of the dream: to act on the hint of the dream.

Now in 2013, I can look back on this piece of my history and see the world of the lighthouse as a steady beacon in a sea of chaos, itself focused on the future as the stormy seas of chaos crash around it. An aspect of fictional reality has entered empirical reality with its unquestioned reality *as* fictional reality.

Now the question emerges whether this process of creating an unknown future, which later will become a world with its unique history, can be achieved in, not merely of a term of five years, but of a lifetime! This thought needs to be elucidated a little.

An autobiography is a story of a life-time, based on memory. We "look back" and recall our remembered life. These memories are, of course, a mixture of verifiable (empirical) facts, wishes, self-serving beliefs about oneself and others, and downright confabulations or falsehoods. Therapy is of course a method for changing our history, replacing one life story with another, presumably better one. I have had several life stories. Before I went into therapy my remembered history was one of failure. When I learned that the soul "makes honey from all my old failures", my history became one of soul-making, not one simply of misery.[128] I also had a history that was permeated by chronic unnamed fear. Constant stress ran through my body, affecting skin and other organs. Then, I learned that I am a "child of a veteran" and my life-story changed accordingly. I suddenly had a vocabulary that could "explain" my symptoms and give me a way to deal with them. Unnamed fears suddenly had a name and my stress abated. I discovered that I had been living in a world defined by war, fear, courage, failure, triumph over the enemy, power, control, and, of course, violence and death. During the course of my analysis and doctoral program I discovered another world that I had been living all along, with *its* peculiar history. This world is dominated by auguries, portents, suggestions, uncertainties, and magic. My childhood was now remembered another way: my fascination with the Arthurian myth, my desiring to join the Rosicrucians when I was just sixteen; my absorption in stirring classical music such as Peer Gynt; my somnambulism; my mother uttering incomprehensible incantations to me such as "John, the bible never said Jesus is the son of God. It was always the son of Man!" These and other memories gathered together to disclose this world that I also inhabited.

Once I had a dream that simply said, "You are a Knight Templar". I did some research into this Order and was shocked to read that they had made a vow of Poverty, Chastity, and Obedience. Another nest of personal memories gathered around this image as I realized how I had unconsciously lived these vows in my own life. Yet another history, another autobiography!

In all these examples, however, I had been the "victim of fate". I found myself "thrown" into a "pre-given" world, as Heidegger says; only discovering that world (or mode of living) after the fact of its givenness.[129]

It has been only in recent years that it slowly dawned on me that none of these autobiographies has the character of being absolute. My life story is not fixed, which means of course that I am not a" fixity", either. This was very disturbing to me, as one mode of living, or world, emerged one after the other. I felt unstable, disoriented. What does it mean not to have a fixed life history? That is how we can tell others who we are. In 2011, I endured a crisis, a kind of death experience that lasted for about a year. During that entire time I could barely move physically and was "forced" to write. In my attempt to understand this vexing question the fluidity of one's history, or history in general, I wrote out the following "poetic" piece.

David is the fictional character who gives me just enough distance to write this material down, without getting caught by it again.

THE COMING STORM

Storms often begin softly, with a whisper in the night, like the quiet movement of a butterfly wing. Eight years into David's sojourn as a teacher at the Catholic school, he had a dream:

> Sigrid returns. I did not think you would come back. So you really do love me then—of course I do. At school, a young woman working in a cafe. We feel intimate. I would have a relationship with you if I were 40 years younger. All through these encounters with younger women I am going over Einstein's theory of relativity, working out the equation. My mind is working it out as I dream within that mind.

David indeed had had a relationship with Sigrid forty years ago. She was his first love—a love that "married" thinking with the eros/psyche mystery, i.e., soul life. David was Sigrid's maths tutor. He was twenty years old, studying physics and maths at university, and she was fourteen years old, destined to become one of Australia's most beloved actors. Their love, like Dante's love for Beatrice, was not satisfied on the earthly plane, but left an indelible mark in David's heart. She accompanied him for the next forty years, functioning within as his lover, mentor, and initiatrix, while shaping his inner life into visible expression through his writing and other artistic productions.

Her return appearance in David's dream therefore alerted David to a new premonition. The dream was clearly concerned with connecting soul with thinking, as had happened forty years ago but with further refinement on the nature of the thinking that the soul is concerned with. Love and depth are here brought together with an autonomous thinking that thinks itself out ("Einstein") through the human being who participates in the thinking by thinking it. David could not help but be reminded of one of his favourite paintings by Caravaggio:

In this work of art, the love flowing between the angelic being and the human being is palpable while, at the same time, he is engaged in thinking the angel's thoughts as they in turn think themselves out through the human on to the page. Following this reflection, David began to feel a little nervous.

> *Sigrid is my initiatrix. Does this mean I am going to be initiated into a kind of Caravaggio moment? If so who is it that is coming towards me? Who wishes to "enter me, in order to transform himself, long before he happens", as Rilke long ago taught me?*

Whenever there is an initiation, there is a death. David knew this truth in his bones and his apprehension grew. Long experience with initiatory processes also had confirmed for David that they always involved the body. The body seems to be the vehicle for the inscription of the spiritual "message" into the essential depths of the human being. Ancient practices of scarification were not mere torture—merely hurting the initiate was not the point at all. Rather, scarification is a process of inscription that alters the essential being of the initiate, i.e., his definition.[130] The scars that remain are simply "memory devices" so that subsequently, upon his return to ordinary life, the initiate never forgets his spiritual teaching, i.e., who he has now become, in his essence.

In David's case, he had undergone a spiritual process that involved tremendous heat and his skin bore the brunt of it for over twenty years, leaving its scars along the way. His inner work had been to make conscious discernments from within that heat, i.e., to learn its various inflections, textures, intentions, and intelligences.

Am I in for another round?

David nervously sensed a storm approaching.

Outwardly, in his life as a teacher at the school, matters began to sour. His tolerance for the institution weakened. Each day became more of a chore, less satisfying, more arduous. He began to plan a strategic retreat each day by secluding himself in a classroom during the breaks and lying down on his back on the floor, well out of sight. His ordinary commerce with colleagues dried to a trickle and his engagement with the students was minimal.

I'll just earn my day's pay and be out of here.

It was true. David's sole reason for continuing at the school was now monetary. There was no soul nourishment anymore and David knew enough about himself to sense a dangerous situation. If his soul life was no longer invested in whatever activity he was doing, then to carry on, merely on the basis of his ego needs, was going to raise the psychological stakes considerably.

One day, David noticed a small speck of eczema between his right forefinger and thumb. He unconsciously scratched it off. It returned a little bigger, and another one appeared on the ring finger of his left hand. At the same time, his heat returned, leaving him wasted at the end of a day, and his nightly wanderings between 1 am and 4 am also returned. His face began to glow red to the point that his colleagues noticed it.

Over the weeks his eczema grew and expanded all over his body. His scratching released the herpes simplex virus which deepened the wounds, and then staphylococcus bacteria got in. His wounded skin erupted at an unheard-of level of pain and David entered a nightmarish *nekyia*. Luckily he had accumulated many weeks of sick leave and the new headmaster recommended he take all the time he needed at full pay. It was a priceless gift to David and he accepted.

His days turned into a living hell in which he simply wandered from room to room or lay down, in agony. He was misdiagnosed by several doctors and alternative practitioners and so simply had to endure, wrapping his body in towels to hold the bleeding and weeping skin that would not heal.

Slowly, slowly, over the blurred weeks and then months, David's resistance wore down and his inner world exploded into life. He knew it was coming. He had been warned after all. The dreams he received had a particular emphasis on "physicality" and "death":

> I lost my job. I am looking for new work as a maths teacher. Surely someone needs me. I am on a motor bike going along a street the wrong way. It is one way the other way. Someone indicates so and I acknowledge. I

notice my right leg. It is almost eaten away around the bone which is quite exposed. Flesh is hanging off. It has obviously been this way for some time. Well, there is no going for work now. That is over! I am under a tree and a dog comes, sniffing. He goes for my leg. At first I am alarmed then realize it is only food for him. A horse comes by. Now, some people come. They are from the organisation that assists with the passage across. I am relieved and I start weeping. Memories come and I finally remember my son Chris, I wish he were here but not to be. I lie there quietly. I see a skull. It is mine but how can that be? As I turn it slowly in my hands I marvel at how at one time my brain was in there. Now the time is close I feel my breath going and I ask to be taken under the tree to go quietly.

And then another dream:

I decide to kill myself. A bullet in the head, but it does not kill me only knocks out brain functions. So now I am alive but in a very different way. I see Viv, (who killed himself) who tells me that meningitis is next. I move into a flat in an inner city area, almost slum where I will become the "Sage of Underwood" or some such. Kate, the actress from *Underbelly* sings nearby to me and the song is beautiful; just beautiful.

David lay there quietly under the gently swaying willow. He was dying. And he knew it. All resistance was gone now. His exposed brain was thoroughly infected with the bacteria that had rapidly invaded through his nose, once the meninges had broken down.

He could gather himself enough to reflect. After all he had nothing but time on his hands, i.e., until time ran out. He noticed that his dreams had a definite emphasis on the brain and its demise.

And indeed here I am with meningitis, on my last legs.

But he also knew that dreams are self-movements of the objective psyche as reflected so often in the "muddied waters" of the subjective psyche of the dreamer. That is to say, dreams are first and foremost movements of the soul as yet implicit (in the background, the not-yet-become) but determinative in the sense of catching us in those movements as they seek materialization or realization in the ordinary world of matter.

So, ever curious, even while he was dying, David began to think.

What is the soul up to in presenting such death imagery while at the same time my body is reflecting those images, in actuality? Here I am dying, alone under this tree with a rotting leg, and a skull, apparently my skull, lies on the grass beside me.

David was familiar enough with the current advances in neuroscience to know that modern consciousness exists only as inextricably linked with the brain and the central nervous system. Some researchers go as far as claiming to predict what we think by simply looking at a MRI scan and observing the section of the brain that "lights up"! David's dreams with their focus on the brain's demise could therefore be addressing a soul movement that includes a death of that brain-linked consciousness.

A death must be undergone! And death is final!

Yet both dreams point to a form of existence in which the link between consciousness and the brain is severed. The first dream showed David contemplating his own skull, the skull that once housed his brain. The second dream explicitly described David as being "alive but in a very different way".

David then remembered an article he had read in TIME magazine.[131] The issue was devoted to current research exploring the ties consciousness has to the brain with the predominant conclusion that, without the brain, consciousness ceases to exist. The particular article that David remembered was a counter-example to the prevailing wisdom. The author is an orthopaedic surgeon who describes a patient whose brain had already been destroyed by cancer and yet he woke up to say goodbye coherently to his family.[132]

David was next drawn to the disturbing image of meningitis appearing in the dream as an ominous hint of what was to come "next". Meningitis is a disease in which bacteria or virus invades the meninges, the membranes that cover and protect the brain tissue. There are three layers: the *pita mater, arachnoid mater,* and *dura mater*—tender mother, spider mother, and hard mother. David was jolted when he read this description.

> *My entire brain, my thinking depends on, and is protected by, these three aspects of the mother. This quite ordinary form of thinking, i.e., reflective knowledge is always "of the past" because it is reflective. And this knowledge is thus petrified, frozen, not living. Of course, petrifaction and reflection irresistibly invoke the image of the gorgon, Medusa who like the triune meninges of my dream lies behind all such knowledge and its petrifying effect on living process.*

David then fell asleep again and dreamed:

> Early morning in the city, few people around. Some
> trams sidle into their station, ready to start the day. I
> drive into a bay. I will follow them. They start off and as
> I follow the road gets more and more rocky and narrow.
> Stones become boulders and all my forward motion is
> impeded. I get anxious and fearful . . . Then in the city,
> the broken down part, I see huge cranes lowering a long
> horizontal piece of stone into place. It is an art work
> called the "petrified Christ".

As all movement is constricted, hampered, and finally brought to
a halt, with fear reaching the level of terror, the ultimate image is
displayed, the petrified Christ, as a work of art.

Following this dream, David then remembered an equally shocking
picture that he had received from a friend, called the *New Pieta*.

Carved in fossilized wood (petrifaction), this new Pieta stands in stark contrast to its predecessors, such as Michelangelo's:

David saw straight away that the *New Pieta* shows the mother ineluctably releasing her son to the grave where we as observers must follow. We are no longer held by her in pity in kind of suspended condition between life and death. It is the final release from the mother who no longer seeks to protect, holding death's claim at bay.

Death's claim is now absolute!

And death's claim on me is now absolute!

David's meninges were now no longer protecting his brain-based consciousness and he was being released to his death. The connection between the knowledge gained by this form of consciousness and the mother whose petrifying stare reduces all living processes to stone lingered in David's musings as he lay quietly in his bed of grass, his breath becoming fainter.

He began to remember episodes from his past. He allowed the images to parade before him, as friends might come by for a visit to the departing one. They were shards, fragments, seemingly no longer held together in a contrived continuity by a self-edifying ego. They came in whatever order, or disorder . . .

As they arrived, first in a trickle, David discovered that he could "ride" one, if he chose, on a basis of attraction or aversion. When that happened, his present state of dying, under the tree where he had been placed, retreated as if receding down a long tunnel and he would become the memory, reliving its feeling, its consciousness.

And so he "woke up'" in a class room.

No! You are wrong! You are all wrong! The forces acting on that object sliding down the inclined plane resolve into these partial forces, not those! I'll prove it to you. I am going to send the entire problem to someone at the University of Queensland and we'll see what he says.

Laughter, Mocking!

Einstein!

Dear John, thank you for sending me this problem about mechanical forces. As you can see from my diagram, your construction is not quite right. The forces rather resolve this way when we place the co-ordinate system on the inclined plane . . . yours sincerely, Dr . . . .

Humiliation!

Michael McRobbie! Fat, the butt of many jokes . . . always trying to belong! I don't mock him. I want to be friends. Why doesn't he come over to my place? I always go to his. He wants to be with Wayne Rubenstein, who always rubbishes him, sparing no pains to humiliate him publically . . .

University of Queensland! I love this place. Physics, Maths, conversations, arguments, study!

Michael, I bet you don't know . . .

Well Woodcock all that depends on truth. What is truth, Woodcock?

Silence.

My god, he knows something I do not. He protects himself against the "Rubenstein attacks" with knowledge. He must be studying philosophy. Now I can see how to protect myself against humiliation. I won't be caught off guard again. For starters, I am going to learn a word every day from

*the dictionary. And, I am going to strengthen my stomach
muscles. You can never tell when someone might come at you
with a good kick . . .*

The shard drifted away and David looked up at the overarching
branches of the willow that sheltered him so lovingly in his last
moments.

*So that is what I was doing—protecting myself for so long
with a carefully constructed edifice of knowledge. Protecting
myself from what? Humiliation, mockery! At whose hands!?
The Medusa stands behind this edifice of knowledge? I have
pursued this kind of knowledge for decades, drawing not only
from my personal past but the deep past as well.*

Then, another shard! David recalled a dream fragment. "You are
a Knight Templar", it said. He caught hold of this particular shard
and remembered the excitement he had felt when he learned
that the vows that the Knight took were Poverty, Chastity, and
Obedience.

These are my vows! How I have lived them during my life!

Swirling memories of being drawn to junk, cast-off clothes, left-
over foods, looking for money in the gutters, dreaming of wealth
acquired through finding the 1932 penny that was so rare; strangely
shy and modest in all things sexual; first girlfriend as late bloomer
while at the University of Queensland; eager to obey authority.

Just tell me what to do!

More shards arrived.

Our past goes further back than the 14th century.

David had engaged with the theory of evolution and its geologic time, aligning himself with those who understood evolution as a simultaneous evolution of consciousness and world. He came to understand that present day consciousness is an outcome and a transformation of former states of consciousness and their correlative worlds. For example he marvelled at the paintings found in Southern France, over 30 000 years old.

What form of consciousness did we have then?

David could feel the old excitement as he recalled the years of study he had given over to the study of the mutual evolution of consciousness and the world, focussing on what happens to each when a transformation occurs.

Now the memories were losing their grip on him. They gathered around his bed of grass under the old willow tree, but their hold him was now tenuous at best.

He began to realize that these memories were indeed shards. Any meaning they had was an invested one.

This must be why we are constantly revising our history texts, our theories of evolution etc. Why, we even revise our personal histories under the influence of therapy or education.

David realized that the meaning-making factor must therefore lie within us! When we take up any shard, be it personal history or stretching into geological time, and "find" its meaning, that meaning must have arisen from within us in the first place. So, deep within our almost obsessive preoccupation with the past and within the myriad self-serving interpretations of the past, must be an impulse to come to know the Being from which we emerged, in the form of our modern day consciousness. Naturally we first find it appearing outside us as a perception of the world. Usually a culture favours one interpretation or another and this passes as the "truth". But really this kind of truth is nothing more than an official narrative that serves that culture's need to explain its own origin in an extroverted fashion.

Another interesting question arose for David. What happens when an individual arrives at an understanding of this curious manufacturing of meaning of "the past"? What happens if this individual no longer wishes to favour any interpretation of the past?

Let the shards remain shards!

No sooner had these words left David's mouth when a gentle breeze sprung up and began to move the willow branches softly. Like so many leaves, the shards of memories that had gathered around him, as he lay there dying, began to tremble and whirl.

As the late afternoon sun broke through the thick canopy, it seemed to resolve itself into a form. David saw a pair of wings folded forward and eyes that were staring backwards as the light-being, for that surely what it was, began to surge backwards. Its unearthly eyes were fixed on the shards that were gathered there, drawing them together in what became a torrent of glittering light fragments, likewise surging backwards so that angel and shards were moving ever apart, with an increasing velocity, yet the whole scene danced in stillness before David's eyes. He heared a dull roar as this catastrophe gained momentum. The angel, moving ever towards the future backwards had its eyes fixed unwaveringly on the shards of the past as its thundering wings beat the torrent into a frothing ever-departing storm wave.[133]

The roar became a cacophany on David's ears and the light gathered in intensity until all he could see was a blinding river of shattered light forms.

And then, David died.

Only now, two years later, do I get a glimmer of what that piece of writing might mean. I was in the process of discovering that my personal history is not fixed, that there are many such stories that form one's remembered life, none being absolute. We are only subject to fate in the sense of being formed by what "inevitably" happens to us during the course of our lives, if we cannot find our way to the various "originating" images (possible futures) that then become our future through our enactment (or unconscious acting out) and then, later upon reflection, becoming our remembered past(s). If we can make this discovery then we learn that we do not necessarily just have one history or one autobiography which defines us. History "through the blood" (as for our ancestors) was of course determinative and carried by the family name. We are now free to invent ourselves ever anew, according to the possible future(s) we choose when they penetrate, as well as *the way* we choose (Williams' purity of desire).

This must mean that, in our essence, we are now simply a "clearing", content-free.

The "artist" therefore is one who can freely choose a possible future, which will later become his history, when he looks back. My next essay explores this proposition, not just over the duration of five years (see *Lighthouse at the End of the World*, above) but over a lifetime. As with the previous essay, I begin with an aspect of fictional reality that penetrated empirical reality and an inception took place.

 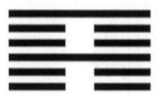

John C. Woodcock

I have consulted the *I Ching* for over twenty years. I use the yarrow stalks method of generating the hexagram which takes about twenty minutes and allows me to settle into the question. I have a kind of discipline about asking for an oracle from the Old Man. I only approach him when I feel I have run out of my own resources. This restraint is based on my rather deep conviction that wisdom can only approach when the ego is sufficiently open and transparent, able therefore to distinguish between its own concerns and the voice of the other. This happens to me when I truly feel I can no longer address my situation from the ego alone.

I then spend some time in formulating the question, making sure that the question does not merely reflect what I already know and secretly want affirmed. A question worthy of the Old Man's attention is one that is relatively purged of personal desire. When I have asked for an oracle in this way, the reading has profoundly affected me and the image has formed the basis of subsequent action, lasting for years before I need to ask again.

In 2006 I arrived once again at the point where I felt ready to ask for wisdom. I asked this question:

What is my current situation and what does the future hold?

The hexagram I received was *The Wanderer* and it had one changing line from which emerged the hexagram of *Stillness*. The Old Man had given me an image of my life's history up to date and an image of what will emerge from it.

The image of the *Wanderer* had appeared once before, in 1998 (see essay, *Lighthouse at the End of the World*) and as before, it penetrated. An inception occurred and images, thoughts, memories began to flow.

As I kept writing, each fragment began to call forth another with a definite feeling of being drawn towards a meaning, as yet hidden.

A momentum started up and I was drawn towards an unknown future. Remembered events in my life, experienced initially as fragments, gathered. I decided to remember whatever I could of my entire personal history, following the method of this, my "art form" i.e., by allowing the images themselves to lead the way.

And so, a poem fragment began this journey:[134]

> Our birth is but a sleep and a forgetting:
> The Soul that rises with us, our life's Star,
> Hath had elsewhere its setting,
> And cometh from afar:
> Not in entire forgetfulness,
> And not in utter nakedness,
> But trailing clouds of glory do we come
> From God, who is our home:
> Heaven lies about us in our infancy!
> Shades of the prison-house begin to close
> Upon the growing Boy, . . .

Being born an only child is bad enough! Although the story goes that you get all the attention from your parents, the fact is you also miss out on a lot, like siblings with all the feelings and experiences that sibling relationships can bring. Unlike other "only children" however, I had to compete with the presence of several imaginary cats that my mother and stepfather included in our family. As most children do, I enjoyed a kind of innocent acceptance of the reality of these "siblings" although I did not feel part of that family at all. I simply accepted the fact that on occasion, my parents would speak about these cats in an atmosphere of amusement that comes with collusion in a secret—or even a *folie a deux*! It was only years later that I was able to associate the presence of the cats to the repeated miscarriages that my mother endured as she tried to have a child with my stepfather.

In the meantime I had my own little secret. It lay in the recesses of my imagination, hidden in a dark corner. I rarely approached it and asked a question. On the other hand, I never forgot about it. I simply felt and knew that in my family, a murder or some violent act had been committed. With parents who held their own closely guarded secrets, I could not expect any adequate answer to my question. Instead I followed my intuition, putting out feelers here and there, as I went along.

When I was about seven or eight we lived in a small town called Redcliff, a coastal suburb of Brisbane. My stepfather owned a wooden chest which for some reason was stored in our neighbors' garage. Mum and Pop Brumby were the closest I felt to having real grandparents. I loved going over there, particularly to feed the chickens that were kept in a wire cage. It may be the only time I enjoyed weeding the garden because I was in fact collecting food for the birds. I even managed somehow to witness Pop beheading a chicken in preparation for the meal. He missed the vital point on the neck of course and so we watched as the headless monster raced frantically around the yard spilling its blood, and gargling a strangled sound as it struggled to come to terms with its new status of separation. Somehow a child can even take that horror in as simply a fact. Perhaps it is because childhood, quite unlike adulthood, really does accept life being so much more than it can possibly comprehend.

The chest lay unlocked in the garage like a pirate's treasure waiting to be plundered. My stepfather had an uncle who fought in the Boer War. The chest was in fact a war chest, filled with memories of his campaign in South Africa. I especially loved his two ceremonial swords and used them in combat with other boys over the next few years. The soft metal of the blade could not withstand the full force of our clumsy techniques and the edges grew pitted and nicked, just like a sword should look, I suppose.

There were stacks of old letters in this chest and one letter he wrote told how he survived in the desert by eating the local melons that grew wild there. I was accustomed to spending hours alone in my play and this chest was a rich harvest for my imagination. Somehow the chest gave credence to my omnipresent feeling that some violence had been committed in my family. I associated the military with the violence. I also imagined cancer and prison.

Viv, my stepfather was also in the army. He served in the Korean War in 1950, the year I was born. His left wrist had been shattered leaving a huge scar. And he held violence in his body! I learned, as my mother did, that you don't sneak up behind him for any reason whatsoever. When my mother did once he almost laid her out with a punch. Luckily he snapped back into ordinary reality in time and the punch never landed. When I was about twelve, my mother told me that he had disappeared. A few days later he was found hundreds of miles north in Bundaberg, his birth town. He had no memory of his journey "back home". He had entered a fugue state, it seems.

My mother met Viv in Puckapunyl, Victoria. In 1951, my original family had emigrated to Australia. My father, Samuel John Woodcock (Jack), was also in the armed forces. He served in the Second World War in the African campaign and later in Sicily as a driver of amphibian vehicles. He was also a sniper. He served as a simple soldier, rising to the rank of Corporal. After the war he returned to his working class roots as a driver, this being the time he met my mother.

It seems that there was some urgency in their leaving England in 1951. This sense of urgency may have had something to do with a scandal. Shortly after my mother and father were married, possibly while she was pregnant with me, my mother had apparently begun an exceedingly strange affair with Bill, Jack's brother. He called upon her and they had dated, much to the horror of her parents, my Grandparents. It's not clear to me how far they took this liaison but it did raise in my mind the question of my paternity! She did tell me many years later that she had preferred Bill all along and if her Dad (also Bill) had merely whispered "don't do it", she would have fled the wedding. All this resonates with a wedding photo I have which displays a telling gesture in my young mother's eyes: "Wait and see! You have no idea who you have married!"

Jack enlisted in the Australian Army through a London office which of course provided us with immediate accommodation and some measure of financial security and so we all quickly left town. We arrived in Puckapunyl in July 1951 on board the ship Otranto.

Four years later, Jack's meticulous army record, which I obtained only in 2005, held a strange evocative note: "Application for Transfer: For urgent personal and domestic reasons . . ."

Viv was my father's best friend and he had had an affair with my mother. They waited until Jack left for Melbourne one day and fled with my mother and me. Jack returned, discovered his monumental loss through a double betrayal, grabbed a loaded pistol, and chased them. Perhaps this was what Viv and Gwen feared. Jack was a soldier. He had seen action and was a sniper. In his young man's naiveté he had been betrayed by his best friend and his young wife. He had murder in his heart. He somehow managed to retrieve me without killing anyone and returned to his barracks where his commanding officer convinced him to give me back.

I never saw my dad again.

I do have a strange residual memory of that period that surfaced again right now, as I write,

"My mother and Viv are going somewhere together and are leaving me at a home. There is a large white rabbit in the yard. I am playing with him." I now wonder if that memory is showing me a possible path I took to deal with the intense suffering around and in me.

Was I like Alice who followed the white rabbit down a hole into Wonderland?

We relocated to Redcliff in Queensland and when I was about seven years old my mother told me that I was to have a new surname, that of my stepfather, and so I was legally adopted by him. When I was twenty-one, i.e. as soon as I was legally able, my mother took me to a solicitor so that I could change my name by Deed Poll, permanently. She was determined that all ties with my father were to be severed. I did so meekly, not having the faintest idea about the struggle that had been going on around me for so many years.

The only leverage my father had to get me back was to withhold his permission for a divorce and he did so for another ten years until in the early 1960's when he finally returned to England. My mother therefore could not marry Viv. In return for having her will thwarted, she blocked any correspondence from Jack to me. Whenever his name came up, she became filled with scorn and hatred. I came to "know" my father only through the prejudicial eyes of my mother, except for that small persistent intuition that violence or maybe even a murder had been committed in my family...

In 1973, I completed my post graduate training as a teacher and was shortly thereafter to embark on an ambitious project of starting up my own school—The Orwell School—which became the first secondary alternative school in Queensland. During that period, my mother asked me to come with her to England to visit her mother and so, once again meekly, I did. This trip had the unintended (by me) consequence of further sundering my connection with my blood relatives—this time on my mother's side, through, once again, my mother's agency.

Somehow the old hatred between my mother and her mother erupted once again and somehow I became thoroughly entangled in it, though I never knew the content of the dispute. Venom spilled out towards me and my grandmother refused to give me the traditional inheritance from my grandfather Bill. His gold watch and other objects were to be passed on to the eldest grandson. I was effectively disinherited in that small act.

My mother's sisters did write to me from time to time, after that incident, especially Pat who lived in South Africa. I found a kindred soul in her eventually, after another twenty five years, but in the meantime I was cast out from the warmth of blood ties on both my mother's and father's side.

My state of disinheritance, and alienation from my relatives was completed in 1998 when my mother died of cancer. Her Will provided entirely for her latest husband and I received nothing. To this day I know nothing of my mother's financial standing. This knowledge was hidden from me throughout my life with her but I suspect very strongly that the main reason for disinheriting me arose from my decision in 1994 to legally change my name back to Woodcock, my birth name. She was infuriated when I told her.

At the time, the painful stripping away of my connections to ordinary life was also deepening considerably. I was being opened up to invisible realities and bursting forth with poetry, essays, and other creative forms that could give expression to these encounters. I was so captivated by my discoveries that initially I did not notice how marginalized and alienated I was becoming. I came to feel that my old life was over and that nothing would remain. After much struggle I arrived at a point of choice where even the option of remaining here at all became questionable.[135]

My choice to remain and forge a new beginning was symbolized by my claiming my birth right symbolized by my father's name. I legally changed my name and my first important social act with my new name was to become a citizen of the United States as John C. Woodcock.

As with so many fundamental shifts in my life, my return to ordinary life and the restoration of my family ties began with a dream. It was the year 2002 and I was lying on the couch as usual, in a state of depression. I spent many hours on that couch—the very couch on which my son had been born. For the past several years I had been engaged in a struggle to return to ordinary life. My efforts included doctoral studies and getting a permanent job in an institution, the first in twenty years. I felt new significance in ordinary life and this led to a feeling of urgency. It was more than personal survival. I had developed a deep conviction that my experiences in the wasteland would be, well, wasted if I could not achieve a return. Yet all my efforts seemed to get thwarted. I could not avoid a personal bankruptcy and I could not avoid having to sell my home—prime real estate—within a year of buying it. It seemed to me that mighty forces were marshaled against me and that I would surely fail. I simply did not see at the time that these dreadful events together constituted the very mechanism of returning to ordinary life.

During my hours on the couch I alternated between watching TV and falling asleep. In the early hours of the morning, I woke suddenly hearing a voice, a woman's voice. She simply spoke my name: "John!" With the uncanny certainty that comes with intuition, I knew that I was being approached by something new, yet familiar, and that I would emerge from my current despair. I knew equally that I must be attentive to small signs and be ready to follow the hint.

The dream was startling enough but even more so as I remembered my experiences in Detroit, Michigan, between 1998 and 1999, the time I completed my Ph.D. This was also the time I entered a short-lived marriage which seemed to be the instrument through which unimaginable forces were funneled, appearing as insurmountable obstacles to my attempts to return to ordinary life.

However, I now understand that they may have been the very forces required to strengthen me for that return, to in fact create a lighthouse (see *Lighthouse at the End of the World* above).

I named this time my Nightmare. My fear had moved into terror and yet the only guidance I received from my inner world or from outer assistance came in the form of one word—courage! I had no hope and hovered near despair. I felt cut off from everything that supported my life. In the middle of this torment my mentor sent me an e-mail in which he simply suggested I listen to a particular song. It is a song taken from the movie: *The Last of the Mohicans*.[136] The song's lyrics include, "I will find you if it takes a thousand years . . ."

Four years later as I woke up on my couch, startled by the dream voice, a woman's voice, I could only conclude that she had found me and that my connection to the psyche, which had been broken by too much fear, was now restored.

I began once again to follow the hints of my psyche as a path into the future.

Several months later in March 2003, I was surfing the Internet, seeing what possible avenues of employment there may be for a recent graduate in the relatively new field of Consciousness Studies. On an impulse I decided to look up a friend from Australia who I knew was working at a university in Sydney. I e-mailed him and while I was at it, I asked if he knew the e-mail address of one Anita Hansen. He kindly sent it to me after first asking her, and I quickly wrote to her. Anita was my great and confused love in Australia, before I left for the USA in 1979. It was also her image that appeared to me at the start of my Ph.D. program (see essay, *Lighthouse at the End of the World*). She had actually visited me several times in the U.S.A. as our lives unfolded in a startlingly parallel way. For example we were separated from our marriages at the same time. We circled around each other, much as we had done while in Australia. Now we made contact and it was a strong one.

We were both ready!

Within three months I sold my home, paid most of my debts, gave notice at my employment, and paid for two one-way tickets for me and my son. We arrived in Sydney and my return to ordinary life was suddenly free of all resistance.

This path I took was the only one that remained open to me and it was the only one I wanted to choose. All other doors closed firmly and without regret. When this happens I know with a certainty that there is congruence, "oneness" between inner and outer existence.

In 2005, two years after settling back in Australia and one year after marrying my Anita, I woke up with a memory of having been "somewhere" last night. In other words I experienced continuity between my sleeping and waking state, in contrast to the normal event of waking up remembering dreams that seem to bear no relationship to one's waking state. It had the character of my being shown something real:

> I am enfolded by an angelic being who gazes at me with great love and we rise off the ground to the heights of vision. He has the face of Rudolph Steiner. My eyes are directed towards the horizon and I see an ominous and menacing dark cloud approaching—this is our future— it is inevitable and just so. My eyes are then directed away from this foreboding vision to one side where I see a bustling harbor, full of commerce and trade. The word "prosperity" comes and I know this is a premonition of my personal future, taking place on a small scale within the larger vision of possible global catastrophe.

This was a crucial dream-vision for me because, during the 80's and 90's I had been immersed in catastrophic visions of possible futures and could find no reason to go on in the face of such dire warnings. Here I was shown the possibility of going on, even prospering in the personal sphere while holding the knowledge of a larger impersonal menace in the background.

It was also exceedingly interesting to me that "prosper" springs from the same etymological root as "despair". They are two sides of the same coin! In temporal terms it seemed to me that I had moved down through despair to the seed of prosperity. My mentor also reminded me that prosperity associates to Prospero from *The Tempest*. This was quite exciting to me because for years, well before my dream of prosperity, I had been drawn to a song by Loreena McKennitt who puts the closing speech of Prospero into musical form:[137]

> Prospero's Speech
> Now my charms are all o'erthrown,
> And what strength I have's mine own,
> Which is most faint: now, 'tis true,
> I must be here confined by you . . .
> But release me from my bands
> With the help of your good hands:
> Gentle breath of yours my sails
> Must fill, or else my project fails,
> Which was to please.
> Now I want Spirits to enforce, art to enchant,
> And my ending is despair,
> Unless I be relieved by prayer,
> Which pierces so that it assaults
> Mercy itself and frees all faults.
> As you from crimes would pardon'd be,
> Let your indulgence set me free.

Prospero here is recounting his journey from disinheritance and banishment to an island where, although isolated from his heritage and rightful position as Duke of Naples, he gains mastery over magical powers. His condition of alienation opens him to invisible influences. When his place in society is restored, he relinquishes his powers in favor of becoming ordinary again ("what strength I have's mine own"). He even speaks of the despair that can come if that return is impeded. He seems to recognize that being on that island in the play is like being in a dream. One may "wake up" to the fact that one is in a dream state and yet still run the risk of being caught in that state. The applause of the audience is required to "break the spell". One cannot do that oneself.

At the time of my own fascination with this beautiful poem rendered in song I had not reflected in this way at all. Only when my mentor broke the spell for me by naming the Prospero-complex, could I be free to view it from the outside. I could only then gain some knowledge of what I had been through.

My own Prosperic return to ordinary life was accomplished by getting the only job that opened up for me, as a mathematics teacher at a Catholic School in Sydney, in 2004 when I had just recently returned from the USA.

How often a new chapter opens up for me through the appearance of a single, unfamiliar door when all others, based on my past experiences, remain closed to me!

The concerns of school life were so alien to the realities I had been immersed in for so long yet I was forced to engage them. Indeed I found that "what strength I have's mine own". Many times I felt unequal to the task. The very way I languaged the world was alien to what was expected of me on a daily basis. So I discovered that I had been placed in the very context most fitted for re-entry into a world that was proceeding as if the invisible psyche did not exist. And for the first time in about twenty years, I had enough money to prosper.

From within that daily grind a seed grew.

I decided to renew my search for my father . . .

I still had some photos of my childhood and one of them was taken as my parents and I sailed from England to Victoria in 1951. On the back of the old black and white image, my mother had scrawled the name of the ship, *Otranto*. This detail arose along with the curious discovery that I had a cousin on my mother's side living in Sydney. Lee was the youngest son of Pat, my mother's sister. I had been corresponding with Pat ever since my mother died. She was the only relative who immediately responded to my account of life with my mother. Her own story of my mother was equally disturbing and together we gained a mutually satisfying picture of my mother's complex nature and its effects on each of us.

Through Pat and her husband David, I found my way to Anne, also my cousin, who had taken on the task of recovering the family tree on my maternal side. She and her mother Pat told me that they had tried for years to find my dad, Jack, with no luck. I learned however that when he had returned to England in 1961 after my mother disappeared north with Viv and me, he stayed with Pat and David for a while and was considered part of the family. Then they lost contact.

All this recently acquired news rekindled my enthusiasm for finding my father and I began to follow these new trails. The Internet of course has become a valuable resource for locating relatives, living or dead. It seems that discovering one's origins has become a matter of considerable importance to millions of dispossessed individuals these days.

But all trails dried up because I lacked a crucial piece of information—my father's birth date or maybe his death date. The fact that I had changed my name back to my father's name in 1994 of course eased matters considerably. If I had kept my adopted name, so many doors would have remained closed because of the social issue of adoption and locating biological parents. At least bureaucracy was listening to me but I could not provide the crucial data to get me into the system until my lovely wife stepped in.

Anita is a social worker working for the Veterans Department of the Australian Government. She obtained my father's Army records from the Australian Army. The barriers dissolved. Soon I received a thick folder of meticulously kept records of my father's career in the armed forces of Australia.

From these records I learned of the effects of the double betrayal my dad endured in 1955 and which probably resulted in his hospitalization with depression. For the first time in my life I gained impressions of him that were not conditioned by my mother's hatred. And I obtained his birth date! From there I entered the British Registry of Births and Deaths to discover that he died only a few months before I had begun my search, i.e., on May 15 2005. Curiously my mother had died on May 14, 1998, seven years earlier.

I had missed my dad by only a few months.[138]

I found out that he died at Worcestershire Hospital from complications arising from a lifetime of smoking. He developed gangrene and at his age it was inoperable. I called the hospital and a kindly social worker assisted me in locating the funeral home which had taken care of his burial. I talked with an employee there who struggled with releasing any information over the phone but did tell me his next of kin: his wife's name was Gwendolyn! I almost dropped the phone. That is my mother's name. I felt instant confusion. Why would he name my mother as next of kin? I blurted out that my mother's name is Gwendolyn and my informant seemed unsurprised since I had, after all, identified myself as his son. She went on to drop another bombshell. Who arranged his funeral service? Why, his daughter did.

Within a few days of discovering my father had died I discovered I have a living sister, whose mother, it turned out, was also called Gwendolyn.

The funeral director of course would not release any details over the phone but by now I was unstoppable. I found out my dad lived his remaining years in Droitwich, and simply by looking in the local phone book via the Internet, I found one Jim Woodcock who indeed was my last living uncle. My father had three brothers and one sister and now only Jim is left (2005). We struck up an immediate friendship and it turned out Jim had completed a lot of work on the Woodcock lineage. He also told me more about my sister and, as well, Jack's marriage which seemed in an uncanny way to be a repeat of his and my mother's. When I did finally talk to my sister we had an immediate and strong connection with surprisingly similar descriptions of our mothers.

More than this though, over the following weeks my cousins and various nephews and nieces appeared in a kind of avalanche. I was welcomed into the family like a long lost son. I scrambled to construct a family tree so I wouldn't forget who belonged to whom. One particular touching moment emerged when one cousin sent me a photo of myself, about five years old that she had kept all this time. More photos and stories came from Jim and my sister. I felt like a ship that had been listing to one side and suddenly was righted. I felt quite disoriented in a most pleasant way. My self-image was being drastically altered under the amazing onslaught of love and kindness extended to me from all my relatives.

I am no longer an "only child". I am no longer "fatherless". I have an extended family. I am a brother to someone and I am Uncle John to some young people. I now have a history that others know about and respond to. I remember the small shock I received as I perused my dad's Army records and saw where he listed me as his son. There it was in black and white, a record of my presence in my father's psyche.

My sister told me that I had been never forgotten. Although Jack was afraid to talk about me to his new wife, he never forgot me and in fact Uncle Jim told me that they both initiated a long search for me over the years, without success. I had lived in the Woodcock memory during my time of banishment and disinheritance and in fact for my entire life.

From the 1970's through the nineties, the garments with which we move through life, which clothe us from birth on with our cultural identity were stripped away from me, sometimes in the most painful way. I had dreams in which I appear naked, trying to express my truth in public and being chased away; dreams in which clothing did not fit, was lost or was from my past, no longer fitting me. These soul realities corresponded with my not knowing how to function adequately in the world. I dreamed of being flayed, sitting on a chair in a dark basement; or, of a body being stripped down to the bones by sharks. I was being reduced to a soul condition which prepares the soul for a direct encounter with spiritual realities.

I found employment where I could, never feeling I belonged anywhere, always "trying on clothing" that did not fit me or in some way distorted what I really wanted to say. I entered different professions, only to leave or get tossed out. My creative impulses were channeled into social forms that were already conserved in regulations or traditions and so I always felt distorted. Although I "performed" well at whatever I put my hand to, nowhere did I feel "at home".

I was a wanderer.

At the same time, I was opened to the spirit. The "removal of garments" was for me a living symbol for stripping away my attachments to outer life. I did not go easily into that good night. For years I was almost obsessive about keeping documentation about my legal and social identity (passport, Deed Poll, birth certificate, professional licenses, academic transcripts, degrees, letters of recommendation which were over ten years old, brochures of my workshops, lectures, and on and on) while at the same time I became more and more alienated from the community. I lost my marriage, went into bankruptcy, lost my home, gave up my professional licenses, refused to work in any institution, so was mostly broke, and lost all connection with my family on both sides.

I wrote a poem expressing this condition:

Until I Surrender

living a life of hopeful anticipation
but the foundation of the house was rotten
bursts of scattering activity
plunges into mindless blackness
edifice crumbles at last

clutching to possessions
thieves come in the night
room laid bare
grasp at career
guard dogs bare their teeth
no entry here

family and home
slowly debts
the weight of saturn
cast into lead

my son visits during the week
weeds grow head high on the land
office built with my own hands
stands empty

family career community
husband father teacher writer
all gone

discredited
unwanted
inadequate

all failures

wind accepts the offering of my wallet
left carelessly on the roof of my car
there goes my identity
turning to my body and psyche
instruments of pleasure for others
never mine at all

nothing left

yet more to hang onto

dreams feelings memories
concepts of reality
god as a concept
merciless insistence!
these are taken too
sitting in the front seat
bowed over the wheel
despair
nowhere to go

crazy mexican breaks into my truck
looking into his eyes
I see what i do not want to see
nobody home!
he returns later to finish the job
let him go
he must be god's angel

lying on my back
beyond despair
now well into sheer terror

abyss opens up below
crying out to mother for support
there is . . . something
point dot hypothesis

brief excursion into the beyond
yields a non dimensional
but real other
my very existence is now based
on this tiniest of tinies

how the merest terror-filled glimpse
into the abyss
can yield so much!
quite an achievement!
i get the point
only to miss it entirely
still clinging to heroic knowledge

and so you come

what despair and terror began
love completes
you love me until i surrender
abyss . . . is life!
i know not
but i love

This poem is only one of an outpouring of creative impulses that
lasted several years. I was in an ecstatic ferment and worked hard
to give expression to the mighty flow that had started up and
intensified the more I was marginalized. The more I was stripped

away of any garments that society had made for me, the more I was opened up to direct encounters with spiritual reality.[139]

> For weeks I experienced a flooding of my body with a kind of nectar that produced an ecstasy in me. I could smell flowers or sweet fragrance in the air. I felt I had grown a pair of wings, palpably, concretely. The erotic intensity was such that I would lay down for hours as a fount of glorious liquid fire poured into me. Many dreams came, and visions, too many to recount here but the flood swept away everything that I had so far assumed about life, the human condition and its limitations. I was given experiences of a concrete nature, whose reality could not be questioned at all and yet which could not possibly be reduced or interpreted back into known categories of experience.

These experiences taught me of my spiritual origins, that there is a spiritual aspect of my human totality that belongs to and has emerged from the spiritual realms and is at home there. I also learned that making this discovery while embodied can involve the most terrible suffering.[140] In our incarnate state our desires are directed outwards in the service of life, albeit unconscious life. When we are turned inwards, reality also turns inside out and so desire appears on the outside directed towards us. I thus discovered myself as an object of desire—desire as an image, and I was stripped of any garb that would direct my attention to the outer material world. Thus I was shown the true state of affairs. Becoming an object of desire involves interpenetrating with spiritual powers whilst having a finite body. Suffering thus is the experience of a limited being filled by these powers.

My return to my familial origins was thus in effect a "return from the dead". Not only had I discovered my spiritual origins from above (the future), but now I was reunited with my blood origins, from below (the past). These two streams were re-uniting in me in a way that produced some very difficult effects.

Throughout 2006, I had a series of dreams that showed me trying to do my work in the world but having great difficulty finding the right clothes to wear. I try on clothes from my own past, clothes that belong to others, none of which fit. I found this very frustrating in the dreams. I could not get on with my "work" as a teacher. I also had a remarkable dream which linked my own participation in an incarnation process with that of one Walter Benjamin. The dream showed that a book comprised entirely of quotations had been completed. Following the dream I was startled to read that Walter Benjamin had spent his life collecting quotes just as I had and he wanted to create such a book, without commentary.[141]

The idea underlying such a creative activity is this: modern life is in fragments but with a proper attitude (he called it the flâneur) he could gather fragments to himself in such a way as to reveal the hidden thread linking them and placing them uniquely in this historical moment. In this way the shattered meaning underlying the fragmentation in our modern life could be revealed to the flâneur.[142]

From these dream hints I began to see the movement in my own life in a fresh way that was quite depressing. I had a wealth of visionary material within, waiting as it were to find its way into world, pressing hard upon me, in fact, heating my body, and leaving my skin in a painful itching condition that was unbearable at times.

On the other hand my outer life had been reduced to the bones and any attempt to return to outer forms that were conserved (from the past) or which belonged to others was thwarted by a deeper intentionality. I had all the raw material, but how to bring it into the world? The necessity to do so was clear. I dreamed of assisting a birth—a baby was born and there was a rush of enthusiasm. He came in fresh and pink and naked—a beautiful birth. Then immediately I dreamed of an uncompromising death. A black and white bird appears as a judge over life and death and an animal carcass falls from the sky, without its skin. Could this be what was left after a sublimatio process, and which had to go to its animal death? An animal dies and a human is born. This is an image of a transformation.

My depression deepened as my skin condition worsened over the months. The death image in my dreams also alarmed me. In my outer world, I concluded that I would not seek any other job in an institution, or rework my resume one more time, in order to distort myself to fit an institution. I would not try to fit myself in any other clothes. My present job as a mathematics teacher at the Catholic school was a temporary gift to me, helping me stabilize financially and the holidays that came with the job gave me the time to reflect and work on my inner life. It would be my last position within any organization.

Even with all the hints from my dreams, I was stymied, unable to rely on past forms to bring in my spiritual treasures and not knowing how else to proceed, or where to turn for help.

During all this uncertainty, I continued to deepen my connection with my sister and with my ancestral line. With Uncle Jim's considerable help, I found my way to one Henry MacDonald in the USA. He was a distant cousin who had traced his own line back into the Woodcocks and even posted it on his web site. In another strange turn of events, it turned out he lived in the Seattle area where I had lived for twenty years without knowing of his existence. With his and Jim's help I was able to construct a family line back to the 18th. C.

My son Chris and I descend from a line starting from one Daniel Woodcock, born 1778. His son was Samuel Woodcock whose wife gave birth to eleven children. Five died within the first two years of their lives, one of whom was named John Woodcock. My ancestors mostly lived in Chester, England, or around the Midlands as my father did.

Uncle Jim sent me an old photo of my great great grandfather, Samuel Woodcock, standing out in front of his shop with some of his children and perhaps his wife. Standing there in front of his little shop in Chester, Samuel portrays those last remaining vestiges of human dignity captured so well in 19th C. portraits.

As with my parents' wedding photo this one was very psychoactive for me. But it took months for me to realize that the most obvious feature of this photo held a mystery that was very relevant to my own life as I had struggled to give it form over these many years of "banishment" from and return to my father's family.

I have known for some time, through listening to others' stories of their own families, that there is a special bond between grandparent and grandchild. They are at the opposite ends of the human life span. The child is just "coming in" as it were, and the grandparent is on his "way out". So they each can relate to each other in their spiritual beings. The grandparent often in fact transmits something of the spirit freely to the grandchild, a gift, unencumbered by the usual parental concerns that produce conflicts between the child's spiritual freedom and the necessary limitations of material existence. A grandchild can thus find an undiscovered meaning in his own soul life, laid out in the enthusiasms of the grandparent's life.

So, here I am, struggling over the years to face the consequences of having my outer attachments stripped away, exposing me to spiritual treasures and at the same time enormous dangers, while being turned inside out. This process was captured as I said in images of having my clothing taken away, appearing naked etc., followed by a return in which I was faced with my utter poverty and destitution and nakedness in bringing back some of the treasure to material life. This was portrayed in my dreams with images of clothing—unable to wear clothes from the past, trying unsuccessfully to wear clothes belonging to others, and so on.

And there is my dapper little great great grandfather standing dignified, with his children and wife, in front of his little shop in Chester. The shop front says "J. Woodcock" and under that his occupation: *Tailor*!

My ancestor was a tailor! The penny drops!

My imagination began to weave around this extraordinary connection I had made with my ancestor the tailor. I returned to the photograph and saw another astonishing detail. Next to him is a little boy with a suitcase as if he were about to embark on some sort of voyage or adventure. My psyche was excited by the connection between the tailor and a voyage or journey or adventure. I knew that his son William had travelled to the USA and that my grandfather was a sailor, a submariner to be exact. My father also was an adventurer, traveler, and indeed so am I—wanderers, all.

I then remembered my long interest in fairy tales that feature a little tailor. In particular I loved Grimm's version. I had wondered for years what qualities the tailor possesses that the human soul uses for its own purposes, i.e., to express soul qualities interpenetrating with other soul qualities within the dramatic structure of a story. I went once again to the Internet and found this version of:[143]

The Valiant Little Tailor

A tailor is preparing to eat some jam, but when flies settle on it, he kills seven of them with one blow. He makes a belt describing the deed, "Seven with one blow". Inspired, he sets out into the world to seek his fortune. The tailor meets a giant, who assumes that "Seven with one blow" refers to seven men. The giant challenges the tailor. When the giant squeezes water from a boulder, the tailor squeezes water (or whey) from cheese. The giant throws a rock far into the air, and it eventually lands. The tailor counters the feat by releasing a bird that flies away; the giant believes the small bird is a "rock" which is thrown so far that it never lands. The giant asks the tailor to help carry a tree. The tailor directs the giant to carry the trunk, while the tailor will carry the branches. Instead, the tailor climbs on, so the giant carries him as well.

The giant brings the tailor to the giant's home, where other giants live as well. During the night, the giant attempts to kill the man. However, the tailor, having found the bed too large, sleeps in the corner. On seeing him still alive, the other giants flee.

The tailor enters the royal service, but the other soldiers are afraid that he will lose his temper someday, and then seven of them might die with every blow. They tell the king that either the tailor leaves military service, or they will. Afraid of being killed by sending him away, the king instead sends the tailor to defeat two giants, offering him half his kingdom and his daughter's hand in marriage. By throwing rocks at the two giants while they sleep, the tailor provokes the pair into fighting each other. The king then sends him after a unicorn, but the tailor traps it by standing before a tree, so that when the unicorn charges, he steps aside and it drives its horn into the trunk. The king subsequently sends him after a wild boar, but the tailor traps it in a chapel.

With that, the king marries him to his daughter. His wife hears him talking in his sleep and realizes that he is merely a tailor. Her father the king promises to have him carried off. A squire warns the tailor, who pretends to be asleep and calls out that he has done all these deeds and is not afraid of the men behind the door. Terrified, they leave, and the king does not try again.

In this story, the image of the little tailor gathers around a certain quality of consciousness that is extolled as a power capable of overcoming brute forces of nature, by turning them against themselves, or by trickery and deception—a kind of magical process. He sews a girdle that reads "Seven at one stroke" which has a magical effect on his adversaries. This is coupled with an irrepressible confidence in his own abilities that seems to defy his diminutive stature, delicate features, and his utter frailty in the face of overwhelming nature forces.

The tailor profession emerged in the Middle Ages and tailor guilds grew in strength and influence from that time, corresponding with a shift in culture, away from merely concealing the body (an object of shame for medieval consciousness) to accentuating various aspects of the human form (the Renaissance) or expressing one's station in life (class consciousness), or one's power and influence in the world, to the modern emphasis on fashion and *haute couture*. Tailors thus became and remain highly influential in society.

And what is it that the tailor actually does? What magic does he weave with his needle and thread, in an art whose secrets were so jealously guarded by the guilds? Grimm's fairy tale gives us a hint about what form of consciousness is involved. Perhaps Parmenides can also give us a hint . . .

When Odysseus overcomes Polythemis, the monocular giant, he does so with a form of consciousness that the Greeks named *mêtis*. As the story goes, Polythemis cries out, "Who has wounded me?" Odysseus replies "No Man" and so when the giant's brothers ask, Polythemis replies, "No Man has wounded me." So they go away thinking him mad, enabling Odysseus and his remaining men to escape. Odysseus is exercising mêtis!

There is no way I can describe mêtis adequately but I can sketch small hints of its centrality in human existence by drawing from a magnificent exposition of the master of mêtis, Parmenides, by Peter Kingsley.[144]

> Mêtis was the term for cunning, skilfulness, practical intelligence; and especially for trickery. It was what could make humans, at the most basic and down-to-earth level, equal to the gods. Mêtis might sound like just another concept. But really it was the opposite of

everything we understand by concepts. It meant a particular quality of intense awareness that manages to stay focused on the whole; on the lookout for hints, however subtle, for guidance in whatever form it happens to take, for signs of the route to follow however quickly they might appear or disappear.

And in the world of mêtis there is no neutral ground, no second chance. The more you let yourself become part of it, the more you begin to discover that absolutely everything, including the fabric of reality itself, is trickery and illusion. Either you learn to stay alert or you will be led astray. There is no pause for rest, or hesitating, in between.

Mêtis is strongly associated with the image of journeying or wandering, as in Odysseus who wandered for twelve years after the Trojan War. Parmenides also was a wandering traveler. Whereas Odysseus travels throughout the Mediterranean, Parmenides travelled to the realm of the goddess, through mastery of the art of incubation. But both needed mêtis.[145]

As any Greek knew, the only way of steering horses or a chariot—or a ship across the ocean—was through mêtis. To be able to steer one had to know all the tricks of the road or the sea, to be watching, completely in the moment. Allowing one's mind to wander was not allowed.

There is a good reason why the imagery of journeying is so important for the language of mêtis. It's because of the speed involved. There is the absolute need to keep focused in spite of the way everything is constantly changing, or appearing to change . . . .

> Whatever mêtis touches is graced with such precision
> that it rarely seems neat and tidy . . . it looks for
> certainty in the realm of uncertainty, not anywhere else;
> is always heading into the heart of danger . . . .
>
> And the reality the goddess is pointing us to is not some
> safe haven of the senses. She is showing us how to steer
> our way through the ocean of existence, how to navigate
> a world riddled with cunning and deception—how to
> find stillness in the middle of movement, the proof of
> oneness in apparent separation.

And finally:

> Mêtis is the one thing needed if we are going to travel
> such a dangerous path without being destroyed by the
> forces we encounter.

So here it is, in one profound concept, images of trickery, deception, illusion, along with journeying, wandering, and encountering dangerous forces, and the possibility of finding the stillness that is reality.

When I had asked the *I Ching* about my path through life, it gave me the hexagram of *The Wanderer* from which emerges *The Mountain*, or *Stillness*. Mêtis is the form of consciousness that belongs to this configuration and thus my own life and at the same time, the unconscious psyche gathers all these same images around the figure of the little tailor as told in the fairy tale, as if to say that mêtis belongs there, too, with him!.

What is it about the tailor that gathers such a profound concept as mêtis around him, as displayed in Grimm's fairy tale? I believe that it is the tailor as a master form maker that gives us a clue here. With the tailor's skill we can become anything, anyone. A stitch here, a tuck there, a clever fold and suddenly an illusion is created. But only the tailor knows how and his secrets were well guarded in the guilds. Mêtis is the power informing this skill, a power that resides in goddess wisdom, a wisdom long forgotten and dismissed by our culture.

A master of mêtis, such as Parmenides, and the little tailor, can both create form and see through it to the stillness that is reality.

And surely the Master is one who can sew his own garments!

While I was undergoing the question of "what to wear" i.e. what form to adopt in order to incarnate the fruit of my own spiritual research, I had this dream:

> Lying with Anita, I enter the in between place consciously. I observe myself with the Dalai Lama. He is on his throne and I am on a chair, looking into each other's eyes. I look deeply into his, great dark wells. There is nobody there, no form. I feel a momentary terror. Then I feel compassion pouring out of that place of emptiness. I am given a mantra: compassion flows through emptiness.

And of course the Dalai Lama wears all the trappings of his office, the spiritual leader of the Tibetans and the leader of the exiled Tibetan Government. I suddenly felt a little closer to that ancient wisdom expressed in the Heart Sutra:

Form is Emptiness, Emptiness is Form!

I no longer doubt that I am being gifted with a considerable wisdom concerning the nature of form and the consciousness responsible for form through the agency of my ancestor the little tailor. In my own journey from wandering to stillness, I am being taught how to "sew my own garment" in contrast to trying on this or that clothing belonging to the past or to others or to this or that profession. Yet I now know that even those attempts belong to mêtis: [146]

> . . . Homer's hero Odysseus—the master of mêtis and cunning "who knew how to be together with people in many different ways."

I even now begin to understand my inveterate habit of quoting others, like Peter Kingsley here, as an exercise in mêtis—adopting his clothing for a while, so that I can converse in that language. Adopting and at the same time seeing through: mêtis!

But the only one who can sew his own garment is of course the tailor, a master of mêtis. I consider this image a gift from my great great grandfather.

I think I am learning now that adopting this or that garb for a while, in order to converse with others is not the problem. Rather, identifying with the garb through attachment is a problem because I have then become a victim of mêtis and the wanderer has become lost in illusion. Neither is the issue to dispense with all clothing for that move is to deny the life affirming quality of mêtis. Rather, I can now begin to play with the image of sewing one's own garment.

This image has had immediate consequences in my life. I feel as if a long search has come to a close. I falsely believed that I was searching for the right form in which I could do my work in the world. This belief kept me in a state of frustration as the form invariably proved to be too tight, ill-fitting, odd-looking etc, distorting what I felt I had to teach. Yet, at the same time I was unconsciously engaging in exactly the right activities that express the gift of my ancestor, the art of practicing mêtis: "how to navigate a world riddled with cunning and deception—how to find stillness in the middle of movement, the proof of oneness in apparent separation".

෨ග

The initial hexagram of *The Wanderer* had penetrated my psyche and generated hints that I followed and acted upon (this time in the realm of writing). In this way I created my future and a new world that I became increasingly involved in. Now, looking back it has also become my past, my autobiography. At the same time I can see a close similarity to the image of the lighthouse—stillness that attracts or warns the wanderer on the stormy seas.

Thus, my personal history was made, once again. At the same time, the purely fictional reality of *The Wanderer* has materialized in empirical reality as my autobiography. This is the way of the "artist". We now have the capacity to be free (through "death"—see my essay, *The Coming Storm*) of history as a fate that befalls us, traps us, binding us to repetition. We can participate in Ereignis, and a new world may emerge, disclosing itself to us through our participation in its happenings which become the new history or memories belonging to that world. How we participate, of course, is of critical importance, as I have already intimated. From these considerations, we can even ask, what kind of world do we *want* to live in? What kind of history do we want, eventually, to have?

At the present time, we are answering these questions only in the sense that the three young people at the Dangerous Ideas conference did.[147] We conjure an image of a preferred future through hope and then set that future as a goal, initiating a plan of action to attain it. This ego-driven methodology dominates our relationship to the essentially unknowable future. It serves the principles of power and control that so pervade the world today, by generating false hopes of attainment which the twin principles then appropriate to their own dark ends.

I also pointed out, through the agency of the recent movie *Gravity*, that such efforts towards the future occlude, for the moment, the fear and terror that is sweeping the world. *Gravity* demonstrates the absurd end-point of such methodology when hope is cleaved to in the face of events of obvious catastrophic proportions that simply cannot be overcome by hope.

Underlying this "artistic" methodology is an intuition that we are no longer simply victims of history, and we can, in the manner of Barfield's "directionally creator relation", participate in forming the future.[148] We no longer have merely to live our lives as "fateful". We have some choice within the given world of contingency.

So far I have shown that a certain telos of Being is taking place in which fictional reality is beginning to penetrate our ordinary empirical reality, gaining equal ontological status as empirical reality but remaining as fictional reality.[149] This is an autonomous process, not human-driven. We could call it the autonomous process of the objective psyche.

While we remain unconscious of our personal tendencies towards passivity, identification, and possession, these autonomous processes of the objective psyche emerge into the world in grotesque forms, as Charles Williams writes so beautifully and graphically.[150] A stark example of this lies in well-established governmental foreign policy strategies. Action on the international stage is based on "worse-case scenarios", images of the future, that, when acted out unconsciously, lead to disaster after disaster. Our identification with unconscious terrors coupled with our desire for power and control brings about "grotesque forms in the world" as Barfield says.

The way of the "artist" demands that the artist is relatively free of such unconsciousness before she can participate with the autonomous processes of the objective psyche. Love can then be the basis of action, as fresh connections (an erotic power) are made between the spontaneous gifts of the psyche that can be received in their own terms, uncontaminated by the unconscious desires of the ego.

I have shown how this artistic participation can work in my three essays above, in relation to two aspects of fictional reality that functioned as inceptions, the seed of two modes of living: *The Lighthouse*, and *The Wanderer*. We can see how fictional reality manifests in empirical reality as a union of telos and contingency, as I struggled to answer the pull of the objective psyche while dealing with my personal unconsciousness (unconscious desires and fears).

My next two pieces explore the way of the "artist" further, with, I dare say, less personal unconsciousness than the previous two. I say this because the actions I took in relationship to these two inceptions were more subtle, less literal, but just as concrete. The worlds or modes of living therefore are correspondingly more subtle. In both cases they involved the world of writing, or thought, exclusively.

I thus began to create my future as a writer.

It began with a dream:

> Three pioneers of depth psychology appear, each
> representing a different comprehension of the nature of
> image, a question that has a long and venerable history.
> I begin to wonder if I could write a book about them
> and their ideas. As I do so, the German word, "Ur",
> starts to repeat itself to me, running through my mind,
> as I sleep. I become enthusiastic about writing a story
> of these three men in relation to image, a simple story
> that brings out the difference in their understanding
> of image. I also am looking around for some electronic
> leads that will help some wires connect to my speaker
> system so that I can be heard better.

I woke up with "Ur" resounding in me. This is a clear moment of
what I call, thieving from Heidegger, an inception—ereignis! The
enthusiasm in the dream also spilled into my waking life but almost
immediately, took a turn away from the dream ego's intention to
write a story about three pioneers in depth psychology. A resonance
had started up and it had the sound of "Ur". It acted on me and so I
acted, concretely.

I started to look around for some "electronic leads". I went to a
search engine and typed in "Ur" and found that the German word
means "original", "primitive" (meaning primary or basic). This
awakened a memory and, according to the way of the "artist", I
included it as the "next step". Years ago I had written an essay, out
of another participatory moment with a possible future, in which I
stumbled onto what I then called the "form of forms", or that pre-
worldly generator of all phenomenal forms. This discovery literally
came out of my hands which moulded clay while my mind was in a
breakdown and I was in a blind panic.[151]

This memory startled me as it seemed I had been, in retrospect,
talking about an Ur-image, as I named it in the moment of

recall—an Ur-image, the original "image" that has to be non-phenomenal and yet which gives rise to all images through a moment of inception. I conceived it as a vortex.

I now had the title of my book. Then, another surprise!

The same search turned up another result. A kindle book had been recently published. It was Stephen King's short story for Kindle, about Kindle, and it was called Ur:[152]

> Book lover Wesley Smith buys an e-book reader and discovers that he can use it to open a window into other worlds and glimpse realities he never imagined . . .

I quickly downloaded and read it. It was a book dedicated to the notion of alternative universes and the possibility of their interpenetrating with our Present. I realized that the idea of alternative universes is a spatial conception having the same weird logic as the temporal conception of possible futures. It seemed to me that King is exploring the same territory as Philip K. Dick, not as his personal experience but as simple fiction.[153] [154]

> Wide awake in his bed, listening to one lonely dog bark in the distance, Wesley began to shiver. His own literary aspirations seemed very minor to him at this moment. What seemed major—what loomed over his life and very sanity—were the riches hidden within that slim pink panel of plastic. He thought of all the writers whose passing he had mourned, from Norman Mailer and Saul Bellow to Donald Westlake and Evan Hunter; one after another, Thanatos stilled the magic voices and they spoke no more. But now they could. They could speak to him.
>
> He threw back the bedclothes. The Kindle was calling him. Not in a human voice, but in an organic one.

> It sounded like a beating heart, Poe's tell-tale heart,
> coming from inside his briefcase instead of from under
> the floorboards, and—Poe! Good God, he had never
> checked Poe!

This startling reference to Edgar Allen Poe released memories of my own involvement with Poe (see *Lighthouse at the End of the World*, above). Suddenly I had the core image of my book—a vortex, along with four main characters: (Ed)ward; (Gar)ry; Allen; and Po'. A flood of images and thoughts flowed and the book was finished in a few days of intensive writing:[155]

> Ur-image is the story of four young friends whose
> routines are disrupted one day by an intrusion of four
> possible futures into their Present, thus shaping their
> lives over time, and finally becoming their actual future,
> but in ways that none of them could have predicted.
> The making of this book reflects a similar process in
> the author. A possible future, in the shape of a dream,
> intersected with the author's Present, and his life began
> to alter in quite unexpected ways, as the dream slowly
> manifested into what became, finally, his actual future,
> the record of which is this story! Thus the author of
> *Manifesting Possible Futures: a new genre of literature*
> further explores an art form which also reflects the
> psychological process by which it comes into being in
> the first place.

As a marginal practice, this art form does not involve imitating what the dream says. Fictional reality cannot manifest in empirical reality that way. The crucial element lies in the inception, which, phenomenologically, is a resonance, or a bell sounding in the artist, quite distinguishable from the elements of the dream content, and then carried forward into empirical reality through an eros-act. This seed of a new world seems to gather those elements from the artist that it needs in order to enter empirical reality, as a story in this instance. Shards of history are woven together in an entirely new way under the auspices of eros. The connections that were being made as I proceeded more deeply with the resonance had a definite erotic feel to them. This is the process by which a new future is forged from the shards of the past, a future created from Love, rather than fear or even terror, as I mentioned above.

Ur-image is thus a manifestation of Love!

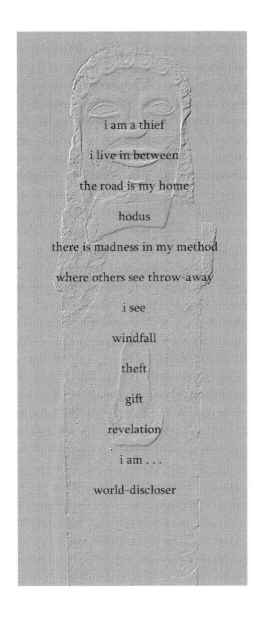

i am a thief

i live in between

the road is my home

hodus

there is madness in my method

where others see throw-away

i see

windfall

theft

gift

revelation

i am . . .

world-discloser

The making of this book began, as usual, with a dream:

> I am with Sigrid. We are in love. Another older woman
> is there and we love each other too. I wonder why I am
> in the position of having to choose between two women
> I love.
>
> Sigrid wants to tell me a dream.
>
> I am in a city. Seems it is falling apart. I stay in a
> large home and try to tidy up, but others come in and
> dismantle the kitchen. I talk to two others who are
> going to tea. No invitation. I start to feel dread. I can't
> go on trying to fix things, it's all falling apart. I walk
> through rubble and notice some Herms. I wonder if
> others see them.

In my essay above (*The Coming Storm*), I speak (through "David")
of Sigrid as an inner figure who has been with me for over forty
years, appearing as mentor, lover, and initiatrix, as she does in this
dream. It seems from the first part of the dream that a conflict in
love generates a desire to "know why" which, in turn, awakens a
deeper desire simply to "tell", and a dream at that—all this taking
place "within" a dream. In some way this erotic, generative process
is initiatory, as I discovered by following the hints emerging from
the dream: Beginning with a conflict in love, if I move with a desire
to "know why", rather than merely satisfying that desire with some
knowledge, I should stay alert to another desire that will awaken
within that desire to know why. This second desire will lead me into
the realm of telling, just as I am doing now. This "telling" appears to
be of the order that Russell Lockhart addresses in his explorations
of the dream's desire, as given to him, yes, in a dream:[156]

I was leafing through Jung's <i>Memories, Dreams, Reflections</i> when a piece of paper fell out. On it, poem-like, was written:

> The poem wants a poem.
> The dream wants a dream.

This dream opened Lockhart up to the startling news that what I am calling fictional reality (his "presentational psyche") has its own desires, or erotic intentions, and these are quite distinguishable from our aims and desires. In the Chapter that holds this dream image, he focuses on the struggle it was for him to release his (and our) reaching out for meaning in favour of following the dream's generative intent for another dream, poem, or "artistic production".

I have already indicated in this book that fictional reality's intent seems to be to penetrate empirical reality in order to impress its reality upon us, as fictional reality. It therefore wants to achieve this on its own terms, not in terms of the categories of empirical reality (subject-object relations; knowledge of; meaning; interpretation, inner/outer, self/other, etc.). Its terms are "artistic" in which participation, expression, and "telling", predominate without concern for the categories that belong to empirical reality.

So it seemed that the first part of my dream, through the agency of Sigrid, has mentored me into further refinement of the way of the "artist" and so with that in mind, I now turn to the second part.

Amongst the rubble of a world, I bend to the task of "fixing it", keeping the old ways going somehow. This effort is thwarted by "others" and there is a lack of any concern for my conflict. A feeling of dread grows. This feeling in the dream acted as a <i>punctum</i> for me in that a psychic movement started involuntarily upon waking—a resonance. According to the method of the way of the "artist" I followed it. Dread is a mixture of awe, anxiety, and anticipation not directed at any object in the world but rather is directed towards the unknown future.

Something awe-inspiring is approaching. Since the dream shows me amidst a collapsing world, I know I am being approached by a new world, with its equally new questions, demands, and tasks—a new mode of being. Then I see some Herms standing upright amongst the rubble and dread gives way to wonder, still in awe, but now with curiosity coming into play, a feeling also oriented toward the unknown future, as a desire to know the unknown.

When I woke up from the dream, I decided to investigate the Herm, knowing from the first part of my dream that this desire to know will awaken another deeper desire to "tell" and that I must follow this deeper desire of the dream, rather than seeking to quench the thirst of my desire to know.

The earliest Herms were simply piles of rocks on the side of the road. As travellers go by they place a rock on the pile, marking their passage. The pile then becomes a marker of the well-travelled road or the seldom-visited one. This was not the Herm I saw in my dream. I saw a rectangular rock with a bearded head and stylized phallus (see poem above). I knew this belonged to Hermes, the god so beautifully brought to life in the words of Kerenyi.[157] I had purchased this book decades ago and I now rushed to my bookcase to retrieve it. I eagerly turned to the Chapter, *The Mystery of the Herm*. The erotic, generative aspect of the Herm is obvious in the phallus but what kind of generativity is this?[158]

> [O]n a black-figure Attic vase . . . we find a black-bearded man who is blowing on a double flute; he is ithyphallic. Four drops of semen are falling towards a large fluttering butterfly, which itself seems to be the first of the spilled drops.

I realized, with a shock, that this is an image of soul-making. Kerenyi is saying that Hermes is a chthonic phallic power that generates soul (the butterfly—psyché, in Greek). I then remembered a passage by Wolfgang Giegerich in which the Herm is discussed: "The act of procreation was not, as for us, a biological event, but fundamentally underwordly . . .)[159]

My dream hints at this kind of generativity when I wonder if anyone else can see the Herm on the side of the road amongst the rubble (showing the possibility of the unseen). Already I am being drawn into the world of Hermes: a world in which ordinary reality is deepened through ensoulment. The depth of the ordinary world is opened up through the generative act of Hermes. Hermes opens one's eyes up to the depth of things.

I spent some time reviewing those aspects of Hermes I was already familiar with—particularly through the *Hymn to Hermes* which sings the child of Apollo: impudent child, thief, transformer, gifter, etc. But then I turned more randomly to other Chapters in Kerenyi's book and my eyes fell on the Chapter dealing with Hermes' association with Silenos and read:[160]

> It is not without good reason that Hermes was supposed to be the inventor of language . . .

> For the great mystery, which remains a mystery even after all our discussing and explaining, is this: the appearance of a speaking figure, the very embodiment as it were in a human-divine form of clear articulated, play related and therefore enchanting, language . . . . Hermes the "Whisperer" inspirits the warmest animal darkness [Silenos—my insert].

The feeling of resonance deepened in me and I knew that the deeper desire to tell was awakening and so I continued on with my investigations, giving up any attempt to be systematic in my

John C. Woodcock

reading. I was now on the trail of a quarry, like Robert Graves' hound.[161]

In the same paragraph, I read how *herma* forms the basic verbal root for *hermēneia*, interpretation—hermeneutics!

Hermes, generator of soul, language, hermeneutics! Wait a minute, what was that book I bought all those years ago and never looked at? That's it! Heidegger's *On the Way to Language*![162] I rushed to get it, opened a page, and stared at a question, "but what does 'hermeneutic' mean?" Lacking the gentle patience of the Japanese questioner, I raced ahead to find Heidegger's answer.[163]

It is difficult for me to capture the complexity of what happened next. So many threads wove together or maybe it was like so many windfalls at my feet, in the spirit of Hermes. Heidegger speaks of hermeneutics in a more original Hermetic sense of bearing a message or tidings. When asked why he stresses this original sense, he replies that it:[164]

> [D]efin[es] the phenomenological thinking that opened
> the way to *Being and Time* for me. What mattered then,
> and still does, is to bring out the Being of beings . . .
> such that Being itself will shine out, being itself—that
> is to say: the presence of present beings . . . . this is what
> makes its claim on man, calling him to his essential
> being.

This thought had broken open *Being and Time* for Heidegger as author and originator of Existential Phenomenology and it also broke open *Being and Time* for me as humble reader, at last, after decades of failed attempts to get "inside" the book. Now, with the help of a Heidegger scholar and translator, *Being and Time* lay open before me.

I discovered I could *read* Heidegger (in translation). His vocabulary previously had been opaque to me: being-in-the-world, for-the-sake-of-which, in-order-to, present-at-hand, ready-to-hand, towards-which, etc., seemed merely clumsy constructions of German. Now I understood that Heidegger had accomplished what no other philosopher before him had. Heidegger managed to find a vocabulary for describing a world that lay "behind" the world of subject-object relations (the Cartesian world). He had found a way to describe the pre-reflective world of background intelligibility that we cope with in a familiar and easy way on a day-to-day basis (I have started to like hyphens now). This language is that of his existential phenomenology and it is a language that can raise this world of background intelligibility, into which we are thrown from birth, into consciousness.

Through his language I had my own version of Helen Keller's marvellous experience of the word acting like a flash of lightning and disclosing an entire world.[165]

As my study of Heidegger deepened, I began to watch with delight how other people went about their business (the business of Dasein) dealing with worldly entities (things, equipment) intelligently and purposively while, at the same time their (and my) subjective minds are concerned with entirely different matters.[166] We are born into a life-world, acculturated by parents, schools, etc., from a pre-given understanding that the world is imbued with meaning—all this with nary a reflected thought! It's a simple as a little baby going to the edge of a cliff quite boldly and stopping at the edge. She understands! Or, when I get out of the chair I understand that the floor will support me and I step confidently, again without thinking about it at all.

Most significantly for me was Heidegger's work on worlds and worldliness—ends of worlds, different worlds, beginnings of worlds, disclosure of worlds, pre-worlds, background worlds, involvement with worlds, etc.[167] I had undergone an ordeal of twenty years or so duration in which I struggled to articulate what was happening to me: spiritual emergency, kundalini experience, psychological crisis, breakdown, madness, etc.[168] These clumsy formulations were a beginning but I needed more refinement. I was trying to say how an undoubtedly personal breakdown could have something to do with a transformation of a world, the end of a world and the birth of a new one.

I finally entered a doctoral program (1997) and managed to formulate my dissertation as: *The End of the World as a Crisis of Consciousness*. I struggled to find a language of existence that got beyond subject-object constructions. Poetry (or poesis) was a major medium for me in this regard. But I did not have Heidegger, until now.

After I read *On the Way to Language* I broadened my research to the well-known depository of modern wisdom—YouTube—where I found a series of talks by Hubert Dreyfus, a scholar of Heidegger's work, at Berkeley. I drank in his introductory lectures for many hours a day until completed.[169] The sense of world-disclosure continued and I bought his books along with that of others, reading with a passion. All that Heidegger was saying deepened and enriched my understanding of worlds. I finally had the refinement I needed. I was indeed in Hermes' world as my dream suggested. I was on the road and windfalls were coming my way at a fast pace as I wandered. I accepted them all.

My desire to know had now given way completely to "Sigrid's" deeper desire to tell. After weeks of reading furiously with many windfalls transforming into the gifts of Hermes and then these gifts being forged into new connections through the agency of Eros, I finally began to write.

This book was completed in two weeks.

Making New Worlds seems to concern the seed of a new genre in which the world and its making are somehow coextensive. I don't seem to be able to say the one without saying the other at the same time.

Ereignis!

ABOUT THE AUTHOR

John C. Woodcock holds a doctorate in Consciousness Studies (1999). His thesis articulates the process and outcome of a spiritual ordeal that lasted twenty years. At first it seemed to John that he was undergoing a purely personal psychological crisis but over time, with assistance from his various mentors, he discovered that he was also participating in the historical process of a transformation of the soul as reflected in the enormous changes occurring in our culture, often referred to as apocalyptic. During this difficult period of John's life, he wrote two books: *Living in Uncertainty Living with*

Spirit and *Making of a Man: Initiation through the Divine Mother.* Both books are now expanded into second editions (2012).

Over time John began to discern soul movement from within present external reality, comprising hints of the unknown future. John's next three books, *The Coming Guest, The Imperative,* and *Hearing Voices,* explore this idea more fully by describing the initiatory process and outcome of a human being's becoming a vehicle for the expression of the unknown future, through the medium of his or her art. John's next two books, *Animal Soul,* and *Manifesting Possible Futures: towards a new genre of literature,* establish a firm theoretical ground for the claim that the soul is urging us towards the development of new inner capacities that together can discern and artistically render hints of possible futures through participation and resonance. His book *Overcoming Solidity: World Crisis and the New Earth* continues this exploration of transformation of worlds. Its focus is on our current structure of consciousness and its correlative world which we call empirical reality. He shows how the development of capacities necessary to discern hints of possible futures involves a kind of violence, due to the "solidity" of modern-day consciousness.

John currently lives with his wife Anita in Sydney, where he teaches, writes, and consults with others concerning their soul life, as a practicing Jungian therapist. John and Anita also work with couples in a therapeutic setting.

He may be contacted at *jwoodcock@lighthousedownunder.com.*

INDEX

A

ancestor 123, 129, 130
animal 17, 21, 37, 121, 145
anxiety 1, 25, 26, 144
apocalypse 25, 68, 72, 73
apocalyptic 69, 72, 151
archetypal 39, 52, 61, 168
Archetypal Psychology 16, 39, 61
art 5, 6, 7, 9, 15, 22, 32, 38, 40, 41, 42,
    43, 44, 45, 46, 48, 60, 63, 83, 89,
    101, 110, 126, 127, 130, 138, 152
Art 9, 41, 45, 63, 160, 166
art form 22, 32, 45, 60, 101, 138
artistic method 61
artists 6, 9, 12, 14, 48, 56
auguries 78
autobiography 13, 25, 32, 78, 79, 97, 131
autonomous 32, 82, 132
avant garde 32
awe 8, 13, 43, 144

B

Barfield 4, 30, 49, 63, 64, 132, 159, 165,
    166, 169, 171, 173, 174
becoming 9, 39, 60, 65, 91, 106, 111,
    138, 152, 175
being xii, 2, 3, 4, 5, 6, 7, 9, 12, 13, 14,
    18, 21, 22, 24, 25, 27, 31, 38, 46,
    47, 48, 49, 53, 56, 57, 68, 70, 73,
    75, 79, 82, 83, 84, 87, 91, 93, 95,
    97, 100, 102, 103, 106, 107, 109,
    111, 114, 115, 119, 123, 125, 128,
    129, 138, 139, 144, 145, 146, 147,
    148, 152, 165, 166, 174, 175

Being 14, 48, 50, 60, 62, 63, 95, 101, 132,
    146, 160, 171, 172, 173, 175, 176
Being and Time 146, 160, 173, 176
Benjamin 120, 159, 174
blood origins 119
body 24, 28, 38, 46, 50, 52, 53, 59, 60,
    74, 78, 84, 85, 87, 103, 115, 117,
    119, 120, 126
brain 86, 87, 88, 91
breakdown 30, 31, 48, 50, 136, 148, 172
butterfly 82, 144, 145

C

capacity 7, 131
Caravaggio vii, 82, 83
Cartesian 70, 147
Celtic 58
chaos xii, 3, 31, 70, 75, 77
Christ 89
clearing 9, 97
configuration 6, 9, 14, 128
consciousness 3, 19, 20, 30, 31, 32, 33,
    40, 48, 54, 58, 59, 60, 62, 63,
    87, 88, 91, 94, 95, 125, 126, 128,
    129, 147, 152, 169, 170
Consciousness Studies 108, 151
crucifixion 38
cultural practice 48
current reality 12, 14

D

Dalai Lama 129
Dante 20, 21, 40, 41, 82
Dasein 40, 41, 59, 147, 175

death 15, 78, 79, 83, 85, 87, 91, 112,
    121, 131
deliberate 19, 32
depression 107, 113, 121
depth psychology 46, 48, 62, 136
Descartes 5, 47, 48, 170
desire 24, 45, 53, 64, 100, 119, 132,
    142, 144, 145, 148, 162, 169
desires 32, 63, 64, 119, 132, 133, 143
despair xi, 107, 108, 110, 111, 117, 118
dichotomy 12, 14, 17, 58
Dick 11, 29, 30, 31, 32, 48, 49, 50, 54,
    56, 58, 137, 159, 161, 163, 168,
    169, 171
doctoral program 65, 78, 148, 168,
    173, 175
dread 142, 143, 144
dream 18, 19, 23, 30, 36, 49, 60, 68, 69,
    70, 72, 73, 75, 77, 79, 82, 86, 87,
    88, 89, 93, 107, 108, 109, 110,
    111, 120, 129, 136, 138, 142,
    143, 144, 145, 148, 171
dreaming 17, 19, 49, 59, 93
dreams 24, 36, 49, 68, 74, 76, 85,
    86, 87, 109, 115, 117, 119, 120,
    121, 123
Dreyfus 5, 6, 8, 47, 148, 160, 166,
    173, 176

E

ecstasies 24, 53
empirical 5, 12, 13, 14, 16, 17, 18, 19,
    20, 21, 24, 25, 28, 29, 30, 31, 32,
    33, 39, 41, 46, 49, 52, 54, 56, 58,
    59, 60, 61, 62, 63, 65, 77, 97, 131,
    132, 133, 138, 143, 152, 168,
    169, 172
Empirical 12, 21, 45, 58, 166, 173
empirical reality 16, 18, 19, 21, 25, 41,
    46, 54, 56, 58, 59, 60, 61, 65,
    132, 138, 143

Ereignis 2, 3, 4, 7, 9, 46, 54, 55, 131,
    162, 165, 171

F

facts 3, 4, 5, 7, 19, 49, 73, 78
fancy 59
fantasy 19, 20, 21, 40, 41, 52
fear xii, 36, 49, 78, 89, 108, 132, 139
fictional 12, 14, 16, 17, 18, 19, 20, 21,
    24, 25, 26, 29, 30, 31, 32, 33, 36,
    37, 39, 41, 45, 48, 49, 50, 52, 54,
    56, 58, 60, 61, 63, 64, 65, 70, 72,
    73, 76, 77, 79, 97, 131, 132, 133,
    143, 168, 172
Fictional 46, 56, 138
fictional reality 12, 14, 16, 17, 18, 19,
    20, 21, 31, 32, 33, 36, 37, 39, 41,
    45, 48, 49, 50, 54, 56, 58, 60, 61,
    63, 64, 65, 77, 97, 131, 132, 133,
    143, 168, 172
flâneur 120
folie a deux 101
forming 5, 53, 63, 132
fragment 93, 100, 101
future ix, x, xi, xii, 3, 7, 30, 62, 63, 64,
    65, 68, 72, 77, 78, 96, 97, 100,
    101, 108, 109, 119, 131, 132, 133,
    136, 138, 139, 144, 152, 165

G

generativity 144, 145
genre 12, 14, 16, 17, 22, 30, 138, 149,
    163, 166
genres 22, 56
Giegerich 12, 17, 32, 39, 40, 41, 46,
    62, 145, 160, 166, 167, 169, 170,
    173, 175
Gothic 14, 56, 70, 71
Graves 56, 57, 146, 161, 172, 175
Gravity xi, xii, 131, 165

H

hallucinations 26
Heidegger xii, 2, 3, 5, 6, 7, 8, 9, 12, 14,
    22, 25, 37, 38, 41, 46, 55, 57, 59,
    79, 136, 146, 147, 148, 159, 160,
    162, 165, 166, 169, 170, 173, 174,
    175, 176
Herm vii, viii, 144, 145
herma 146
hermeneutic 146
hermeneutics 39, 146
Hermes 25, 144, 145, 146, 148, 162,
    168, 169, 175
Hermetic 146
hexagram 69, 100, 128, 131
Hillman 15, 16, 17, 20, 39, 41, 48, 61,
    62, 161, 167, 169, 173
historical 4, 7, 12, 13, 45, 58, 61, 62, 68,
    71, 73, 120, 151
history 6, 9, 14, 48, 61, 62, 63, 77, 78,
    79, 95, 97, 100, 101, 114, 131,
    132, 136, 139, 166, 174
hope x, xi, xii, 57, 108, 131, 132
horror 13, 17, 20, 56, 57, 63, 102, 103
Hunt vii, 42, 43

I

I Ching 69, 73, 100, 128
images 14, 16, 17, 19, 37, 39, 49, 56, 69,
    77, 87, 91, 97, 100, 101, 123, 128,
    132, 137, 138
imaginal 16, 17, 18, 20, 21, 32, 41, 62
imagination 63, 70, 102, 103, 123
Imagination 63
incarnation 63, 68, 120
inception 2, 4, 7, 9, 16, 29, 46, 54, 65,
    77, 97, 100, 136, 137, 138, 171
initiatory 24, 38, 84, 142, 152, 166
inner 5, 12, 13, 14, 30, 37, 41, 50, 61,
    62, 63, 82, 84, 85, 86, 108, 109,
    121, 142, 143, 152, 170

intelligence ix, 126
interiority 13, 18, 41, 56, 57, 62
interpenetration 21, 22, 25, 29, 48, 49,
    58, 60, 70, 72, 74, 75, 168
Interpenetration 59
intuition 53, 102, 105, 107, 132
involuntary 9, 50
inwardness 7, 13, 56, 61, 170

J

Jung 14, 15, 16, 17, 19, 20, 21, 22, 24,
    25, 29, 30, 32, 36, 37, 38, 39, 40,
    41, 45, 48, 49, 50, 54, 56, 58,
    60, 63, 77, 143, 159, 160, 161,
    162, 167, 168, 169, 170, 172, 173,
    174, 175

K

Kerenyi 144, 145, 162, 168, 169, 175
King 137, 162, 163, 172, 175
Kingsley 126, 130, 162, 174
Knight Templar 79, 93
kundalini 148

L

language 2, 3, 9, 12, 15, 16, 25, 37, 39,
    46, 48, 49, 50, 56, 57, 58, 60,
    62, 70, 127, 130, 145, 146, 147,
    148, 165
Lewis 16, 19, 52, 162, 169, 171
life-world 2, 6, 166, 174
Light vii, 42, 43, 44, 73, 173
lighthouse 65, 68, 69, 71, 72, 73, 74, 75,
    76, 77, 108, 131, 174
Lighthouse 68, 71, 74, 76, 97, 100, 108,
    133, 138, 162, 173
literal 7, 12, 32, 61, 62, 133
literature 12, 13, 14, 16, 22, 50, 68, 70,
    138, 163, 166, 167
Lockhart 77, 142, 143, 162, 165, 170,
    173, 175

logical life 62
love 13, 24, 45, 53, 59, 64, 82, 83, 92,
    108, 109, 114, 118, 140, 142
Love 82, 132, 139

M

madness 20, 24, 40, 72, 75, 172
Magical Realism 50
marginal practice 9, 12, 14, 22, 24, 25,
    29, 30, 48, 56, 58, 61, 62, 63, 64,
    138, 167
Marlowe 68, 69, 70, 71, 72, 73, 76,
    162, 173
marvelous 52
McKennitt 110, 174
meaning 1, 2, 4, 5, 7, 12, 25, 26, 27, 28,
    29, 39, 49, 77, 94, 95, 100, 120,
    123, 136, 143, 147
Medusa vii, 88
memory 30, 48, 78, 84, 91, 103, 104,
    109, 115, 136
meningitis 86, 87, 88
methodology x, xi, 20, 62, 131, 132
mêtis 126, 127, 128, 129, 130
mind x, 11, 15, 16, 27, 28, 30, 31, 38,
    39, 58, 61, 82, 104, 127, 136, 143
mode of living 77, 79, 165
mouthpiece 58, 60, 64
Muse 56, 57
mystery 3, 37, 39, 46, 71, 82, 122, 145,
    172
myth 78

N

Nature 14, 54, 159, 163, 165, 172
new world 3, 4, 5, 6, 7, 9, 12, 16, 22, 25,
    29, 48, 49, 50, 61, 65, 77, 131,
    138, 144, 171
Nietzsche 6, 33, 37, 39, 161, 162, 169

O

Oliver 73, 173
ontological 13, 14, 40, 41, 61, 132
ordeal 24, 32, 37, 39, 40, 41, 50, 72, 75,
    147, 151, 176
outer 5, 12, 24, 28, 29, 30, 45, 50, 53,
    72, 108, 109, 115, 119, 120, 121,
    123, 143

P

paradigm 5, 6, 8, 70
Parmenides 126, 127, 129
participate 64, 68, 131, 132
participates 30, 63, 82
participation 30, 31, 48, 49, 63, 65,
    120, 131, 133, 143, 152, 171
past 8, 9, 28, 30, 41, 62, 72, 73, 88, 91,
    93, 95, 96, 97, 107, 111, 115, 120,
    121, 123, 130, 131, 139
penetrates 46, 54, 63, 65
personality 54
phallus vii, viii, 144
phenomenological 29, 146
phenomenology 4, 32, 39, 48, 50, 59,
    70, 147
phenomenon 29, 30, 31, 39, 48, 49, 50,
    58, 62, 68, 70, 171
philosophical double-vision 49, 171
Pieta vii, 89, 90, 91
Poe 20, 70, 71, 72, 73, 74, 76, 138
poetic 15, 16, 39, 61, 79
poetry 15, 25, 54, 56, 58, 106, 173
Polt 1, 2, 3, 8, 55, 162, 165
positive reality 45
positivism 5, 9
possible futures 97, 109, 137, 138, 152
power 6, 56, 57, 58, 63, 78, 125, 126,
    129, 131, 132, 145, 168
pre-given 79, 147
prepare xii
Pre-worldly 1

primordial 8, 37
prosperity 109, 110
psyche 15, 39, 45, 50, 60, 82, 87, 108,
    111, 114, 117, 124, 128, 131, 132,
    133, 143, 165
Psychology 46, 160, 161, 167, 169,
    170, 173
psychosis 28, 36
punctum 143
purity of desire 53, 63, 97

R

Read 60, 77
reconfigure 6, 7
Red Book 14, 15, 16, 17, 20, 21, 25, 29,
    32, 36, 37, 39, 40, 41, 45, 48,
    160, 161, 162, 167, 169, 170
reflection 15, 20, 30, 48, 49, 50, 83, 88,
    97, 171
revelation 15, 29, 50
Romme 26
Rousseau 13

S

Sentimentalism 14
Shamdasani 15, 16, 17, 20, 39, 48, 161,
    162, 167, 169
shard 93, 95
Silenus 145
skull 86, 87
soul 3, 16, 23, 39, 45, 61, 62, 63, 68,
    73, 78, 82, 84, 87, 106, 115, 123,
    124, 145, 146, 151, 152
spiritual origins 119
spiritual process 84
spontaneity 32
spontaneous 32, 132
story 12, 28, 56, 58, 59, 61, 65, 72, 73,
    78, 79, 101, 112, 124, 125, 126,
    136, 137, 138, 173
suffering 38, 40, 104, 119
surface 7, 21, 54, 58, 59, 62
Surrender 116

suspension 37, 38, 39, 63, 174

T

tailor 123, 124, 125, 126, 128, 129, 130
Taliesin 58, 60
technological 7, 9, 57, 62
terror 6, 13, 54, 89, 108, 118, 129,
    132, 139
theoretical thinking 55
thrill 3, 14, 56
Tolstoy 58, 60, 163, 172
torment 38, 40, 108
transfiguration 38
transformation 25, 38, 68, 94, 121,
    148, 151, 152, 166, 172
trauma 27

U

UFO 59
unconscious 25, 36, 37, 38, 39, 40, 41,
    49, 63, 68, 119, 128, 132, 133,
    162, 167, 169
unconsciousness 132, 133
unknown future xii, 77, 152
unnoticed 9, 12, 15
unreal 12, 14, 18, 41, 45
Ur 136, 137, 138, 139, 175

V

victim 36, 57, 79, 130
violence 36, 40, 45, 54, 57, 58, 78, 103,
    105, 152
violent 36, 39, 50, 102
Voices 26, 27, 28, 152
vortex viii, 137, 138

W

Wanderer viii, 69, 100, 128, 131, 133
Williams 52, 53, 63, 97, 132, 162, 163,
    171, 175
Wonderland 16, 18, 105, 159, 167

John C. Woodcock

world x, xii, 2, 3, 4, 5, 6, 7, 8, 9, 11, 12,
       13, 16, 18, 19, 25, 26, 27, 28, 30,
       31, 32, 36, 43, 46, 47, 48, 50, 52,
       56, 57, 58, 61, 62, 63, 64, 65, 68,
       69, 70, 71, 73, 74, 76, 77, 78, 79,
       85, 87, 94, 95, 108, 111, 115, 119,
       120, 121, 124, 126, 127, 128,
       130, 131, 132, 133, 143, 144, 145,
       147, 148, 149, 152, 165, 166, 169,
       171, 172, 175
World vii, 42, 43, 44, 54, 68, 71, 74, 76,
       97, 100, 103, 108, 138, 148, 152,
       160, 162, 163, 165, 166, 167, 168,
       170, 172, 173, 176

Z

Zarathustra 37, 38, 161, 169

BIBLIOGRAPHY

Adler, G., & Jaffe, A. (Eds.). (1975). *C. G. Jung Letters (Vols. 2 (1951-1961)).* (R. F. Hull, Trans.) London: Routledge & Kegan Paul, Ltd.

Augustine. (tr. Pusey, E. B.). (2009).*The Confessions of St. Augustine:* Book VI.

Barfield, O. (1957). *Saving the Appearances: A Study in Idolatry.* London. Faber and Faber.

_____(1977). *The Rediscovery of Meaning.* San Rafael. California.

Benjamin, W. (ed. Arendt, H. Tr. Zohn, H.). (1988). "Thesis on the Philosophy of History". *Illuminations: Essays and Reflections.* New York, Schocken Books.

Borgman, A. (2005). "Technology". *A Companion to Heidegger (Blackwell Companions to Philosophy, Vol. 29).* Kindle Edition. Kindle Location 7565.

Bortoft, Henri (1996-05-01). *The Wholeness of Nature.* Lindisfarne Books. Kindle Edition.

Carroll, L. (2008). *Alice's Adventures in Wonderland.* Eire. Evertype.

Dick, P. K. (1981). *Valis.* London. The Orion Publishing Group Ltd.

_____ *The Android Prophet.* YouTube. Uploaded by TheodoreBrutal.

Dreyfus, H. (2005). "Heidegger's Ontology of Art". *A Companion to Heidegger (Blackwell Companions to Philosophy, Vol. 29)*. Kindle Edition.

_____ (1995). *Being-in-the-World*. *A Companion to Heidegger's Being and Time, Division 1*. Cambridge. MIT Press.

Edwards, J. C. (2005). "The Thinging of the Thing". *A Companion to Heidegger (Blackwell Companions to Philosophy, Vol. 29)*. Kindle Edition.

Emerson, R. W. "The Over-Soul". *Digital Emerson*: A Collective Archive. http://digitalemerson.wsulibs.wsu.edu/exhibits/show/about.

Giegerich, W. (2005). *The Neurosis of Psychology*. New Orleans. Spring Journal Books.

_____(2007). *Technology and the Soul: From the Nuclear Bomb to the World Wide Web*. New Orleans. Spring Journal Books.

_____ (2008). *Soul Violence*. New Orleans. Spring Journal Books.

_____ (2010). "Liber Novis, that is, The New Bible, A First Analysis of C. G. Jung's Red Book." *Spring 83: Minding The Animal Psyche*. New Orleans. Spring Journal.

_____ (2010). *The Soul Always Thinks*. New Orleans. Spring Journal Books.

_____ (2012). *What is Soul?* New Orleans. Spring Journal Books.

_____ (2013). *The Flight into the Unconscious*. New Orleans. Spring Journal Books.

Graves, R. (1994). *The White Goddess: A Historical Grammar of Poetic Myth*. New York. The Noonday Press.

Grimm, J. (2007, April 12). *Household Tales*. Retrieved from Wikipedia: http://en.wikipedia.org/wiki/The_Valiant_Little_Tailor.

Haig, S. (2007). "The Power of Hope". *TIME. (27/01/2007). Mind and Body Special Issue*. Vol. 169. No. 5.

Heidegger, M. (Tr. Hertz, P. D). (1982). *On the Way to Language*. San Francisco. Harper.

Hillman, J. (1994). *Healing Fiction*. Dallas. Spring Publications, Inc.

_____;Shamdasani, S. (2013). *Lament of the Dead: Psychology After Jung's Red Book*. New York. Norton.

_____;Shamdasani, S. (2013-08-26). *Lament of the Dead: Psychology After Jung's Red Book*. W. W. Norton & Company. Kindle Edition.

Hornstein, G. A. (2009). *Agnes's Jacket: A Psychologists Search for the Meanings of Madness*. New York: Rodale, Inc.

Jackson, P. and Lethem, J. (Eds) (2011*). The Exegesis of Philip K. Dick*. New York. Houghton Mifflin Harcourt.

Jung, C. G. (tr. R. F. Hull) (1977). *The Collected Works of C. G. Jung (2nd ed., Vol. 11)*. Princeton. Princeton University Press.

_____ (ed. Jarrett, J. L.) (1988). *Nietzsche's Zarathustra: Notes of the Seminar Given in 1934-1939*. Princeton. Princeton University Press.

_____ (ed. W. McGuire) (1989). *Analytical Psychology: Notes on the Seminar Given in 1925*. Princeton: Princeton University Press.

_____ (ed. Shamdasani, S.). (2009). *The Red Book*. New York. Norton.

_____ (ed. G. A. Adler, & tr. R. F. Hull) (1975). *C. G. Jung Letters (Vols. 2 (1951-1960)*. London: Routledge and Kegan Paul.

Keller, H. (1959). *The Story of My Life*. London: Hodder and Stoughton.

Kerenyi, K. (1976). *Hermes: Guide of Souls*. Dallas. Spring Journal Books.

King, S. (2009). *UR*. Storyville, LLC. Kindle Edition.

Kingsley, P. (2003). *Reality*. Inverness: Golden Sufi Centre.

Lewis, C. S. (1980). *Surprised by Joy: The Shape of My Early Life*. Glasgow. Fount Paperbacks.

_____(2012, 11 29). *C. S. Lewis Lectures on the Novels of Charles Williams*. Retrieved from YouTube: https://www.youtube.com/watch?v=Z5wl34gYz04.

Lockhart, R. A. (1987). *Psyche Speaks*: A Jungian Approach to Self and World. Wilmette. Chiron.

Marlowe, S. (1995). *The Lighthouse at the End of the World*. New York. Plume.

Nietzsche, F. *Beyond Good and Evil*. Found in a blog entry by Joseph Weissman and published on Sunday, September 30, 2007 at 5:27 pm. See: http://fractalontology.wordpress.com/2007/09/30/nietzsche-and-the-unconscious-ethics-desire-politics/.

Polt, R. *Ereignis*. A Companion to Heidegger (Blackwell Companions to Philosophy, Vol. 29). Kindle Edition.

Sutin, L. (1989). *Divine Invasions: A Life of Philip K. Dick.* New York. Carroll and Graf.

TIME. (27/01/2007). *Mind and Body Special Issue.* Vol. 169. No. 5.

Tolstoy, N. (1989). *The Coming of the King: A Novel of Merlin.* London. Bantam Books.

Williams, C. (2003). *The Place of the Lion.* Vancouver. Regent College Publishing.

Woodcock, J. C. (2009). *Transformation of the World.* Bloomington. iUniverse.

_____ (2011). *The Imperative.* Bloomington. iUniverse.

_____ (2012). *Animal Soul.* Bloomington, iUniverse.

_____ (2012). *Making of a Man: Initiation through the Divine Mother.* Bloomington. IUniverse.

_____ (2013). *Living in Uncertainty Living with Spirit.* Bloomington. iUniverse.

_____ (2013). *Manifesting New Futures: Towards a New Genre of Literature.* Bloomington. iUniverse.

_____ (2013). *UR-image.* Bloomington. iUniverse.

_____ (2013). *Overcoming Solidity: World Crisis and the New Nature.* Bloomington. iUniverse.

END NOTES

1   Excerpt taken from Wikipedia entry: *http://en.wikipedia.org/wiki/Gravity_(film)*.

2   With thanks to Russell Lockhart for this crucial conception of the future: "We must each become tellers and doers in relation to what we experience [in the objective or presentational psyche]. This is the new development we are searching for. How little we know that the work we do in this is critical to everyone and the world." See Lockhart, R. A. (1987). *Psyche Speaks: A Jungian Approach to Self and World*. Wilmette. Chiron. P. 55.

3   My equivocal use of this word is to indicate that I do not mean only a formal discipline, but a way of life, a cultural form that is a mode of living, a world that may be in the making, requiring new language to disclose it.

4   See Chapter: *The Herm* for a fuller account of my "meeting with Heidegger".

5   "Life-World" and "way of being" point to the way we actually live our lives, the familiar world that discloses itself through our conduct, or coping, as Heidegger puts it. I will use the word, *world*, for this.

6   Polt, R. "Ereignis". *A Companion to Heidegger (Blackwell Companions to Philosophy, Vol. 29)* (Kindle Locations 6806-6812). Kindle Edition.

7   See Note 4 re: "preparing the future".

8   Keller, H. (1959) *The Story of My Life*. London: Hodder and Stoughton. P. 23.

9   Barfield, O. (1957). *Saving the Appearances: A Study in Idolatry*. London. Faber and Faber. Pp. 69-70.

10 Bortoft, Henri (1996-05-01). *The Wholeness of Nature* (Kindle Locations 968-970). Lindisfarne Books. Kindle Edition.

11 Augustine. (tr. Pusey, E. B.). *The Confessions of St. Augustine: Book VI*. (2009).

[12]   Dreyfus, H. "Heidegger's Ontology of Art". *A Companion to Heidegger (Blackwell Companions to Philosophy, Vol. 29)* (Kindle Locations 388-392). Kindle Edition.

[13]   Ibid.

[14]   Edwards, J. C. "The Thinging of the Thing". *A Companion to Heidegger (Blackwell Companions to Philosophy, Vol. 29)* (Kindle Location 8265). Kindle Edition.

[15]   "Thing" here refers to "equipment", or Heidegger's "ready-to-hand"—an entity that is not just an object of the *physical* world (quantifiable, measurable, isolated from the life-world)—but an entity that is embedded in a world and whose ordinary use discloses the background of intelligibility that gave rise to it in the first place.

[16]   Dreyfus, H. "Heidegger's Ontology of Art". *A Companion to Heidegger (Blackwell Companions to Philosophy, Vol. 29)* (Kindle Locations 7547-7548). Kindle Edition.

[17]   Op. Cit.

[18]   Op. Cit.

[19]   Dreyfus, H. Op. Cit.

[20]   For an excellent discussion of Heidegger's understanding of the linguistics of technology, see: Borgman, A. "Technology" in *A Companion to Heidegger (Blackwell Companions to Philosophy, Vol. 29)* (Kindle Location 7565). Kindle Edition.

[21]   Woodcock, J. C. (2013). *Manifesting New Futures: Towards a New Genre of Literature*. Bloomington. iUniverse. In particular see Chapter: *Tarning and Empirical Reality*.

[22]   Ibid.

[23]   Giegerich, W. (2007). *Technology and the Soul: From the Nuclear Bomb to the World Wide Web*. New Orleans. Spring Journal Books. p.31ff.

[24]   Further discussion of this transformation may be found in: Barfield, O. (1957). *Saving the Appearances*. London. Faber and Faber. Chapter XII.

[25]   Our present way of being is immune from any *initiatory* effect from natural events. Wolfgang Giegerich describes this immunity in terms of a split between natural science and history. See "The Bottomless of

History" in: Giegerich, W. (2008). *Soul Violence*. New Orleans. Spring Journal Books.

26   My own eyes were opened to this marginal practice over a twenty year "spiritual crisis" in which I was drawn in to the whole question of "new worlds". See my books: Woodcock, J. C. (2011). *The Imperative*. Bloomington. iUniverse; Woodcock, J. C. (2009). *Transformation of the World*. Bloomington. iUniverse.

27   See the Introduction by Shamdasani (Editor) for a full discussion of the publication of the book: Jung, C. G. (ed. Shamdasani, S.). (2009). *The Red Book*. New York. Norton.

28   Hillman, J.; Shamdasani, S. (2013). *Lament of the Dead: Psychology After Jung's Red Book*. New York. Norton.

29   For a fuller discussion, see my book: Woodcock, J. C. (2012). *Animal Soul*. Bloomington. iUniverse.

30   Hillman, J.; Shamdasani, S. (2013-08-26). *Lament of the Dead: Psychology After Jung's Red Book*. W. W. Norton & Company. Kindle Edition, Pp. 43-44.

31   For a fuller discussion see my essay, *The Truth of Our Times* at: http://www.lighthousedownunder.com/truthofourtimes.pdf.

32   *The Red Book*, op.cit. p. 323.

33   Giegerich, W. (2010). "Liber Novis, that is, The New Bible, A First Analysis of C. G. Jung's Red Book". *Spring 83*. Pp. 361-413.

34   P. 246

35   Op. Cit. P. 402.

36   Carroll, L. *Alice's Adventures in Wonderland*. (2008). Eire. Evertype.

37   Jung, C. G., (W. McGuire, Ed.) (1989). *Analytical Psychology: Notes on the seminar given in 1925*. Princeton: Princeton University Press. P. 47.

38   For a sustained, unremitting practice of this procedural move of Jung's, see the movie, *Inception* (2009).

39   Jung, C. G. *The Red Book*. Op. Cit. P. 290.

40   Jung, C. G. (1989). *Analytical Psychology*. Op. Cit. P. 96-97. This is Jung's experience of the *Leontocephalus* which has attracted attention in the secondary literature for the purpose of challenging or affirming Jung's concept of the collective unconscious. See, for example, Noll, R. (1992). "Jung the Leontocephalus", *Spring 53*. Putnam. Spring Journal. Pp. 12-60, and Mogenson's rebuttal: Mogenson, G. (1994).

"The Collective Unconscious and the Leontocephalus: A Rejoinder to Noll". Letter to the Editor, *Spring 56*: Putnam. Spring Journal. Pp. 132-137. In this rebuttal, Mogenson notes that for Jung: "It was not the parrellism of the imagery that was of archetypal significance, but his living experience of its numinous power. It was the fact that he experienced an initiation and felt himself to be transformed that was important, not his having been transfigured into the Lion-headed deity, Leontocephalus." It is in this passage that Mogenson notes, without grasping its significance, that Jung is saying that he [Jung] was *initiated*, in his empirical reality, by a purely fictional reality!

[41]   I describe similar personal experiences in: Woodcock, J. C. (2011). *The Imperative*. Bloomington. iUniverse. Pp. 18 ff.

[42]   Op. Cit.

[43]   Woodcock, J. C. (2012). *Making of a Man: Initiation through the Divine Mother*. Bloomington. iUniverse.

[44]   See Kerenyi, K. (1976). *Hermes: Guide of Souls*. Dallas. Spring Journal Books.

[45]   Op. Cit.

[46]   My doctoral program: *The End of the World as a Crisis of Consciousness* was my first systematic step towards giving voice to this strange interpenetration of realities. See http://www.lighthousedownunder.com/doctoral_work.htm.

[47]   Jung, C. G. (1963). *Memories, Dreams, Reflections*. New York: Random House.

[48]   http://www.intervoiceonline.org

[49]   http://www.hearing-voices.org/

[50]   Hornstein, G. A. (2009). *Agnes's Jacket: A Psychologists Search for the Meanings of Madness*. New York: Rodale, Inc.

[51]   Op. Cit.

[52]   Hornstein, G. A. Op. Cit.

[53]   Ibid

[54]   Dick, P. K. (1981). *Valis*. London. The Orion Publishing Group Ltd.

[55]   Jackson, P. and Lethem, J. (Eds) (2011). *The Exegesis of Philip K. Dick*. New York. Houghton Mifflin Harcourt.

[56]   From the Introduction.

[57]   From the Cover (Inside Flap).

58 For a delightful and penetrating discussion of a variation of these opposites (expressed as enjoyment/contemplation), see: Lewis, C. S. (1980). *Surprised by Joy: The Shape of My Early Life*. Glasgow. Fount Paperbacks. Pp. 174 ff.

59 See Barfield, O. (1957). *Saving the Appearances: A Study in Idolatry*. Op. Cit.

60 Dick, P. K. *The Android Prophet*. YouTube. Uploaded by TheodoreBrutal.

61 Giegerich, W. (2010). *Liber Novis, that is, The New Bible, A First Analysis of C. G. Jung's Red Book*. Op. Cit. P.372 ff.

62 Nietzsche, F. *Beyond Good and Evil*. This passage draws out the correlative relationship between empirical reality and consciousness in the modern world. The quote was found in a blog entry by Joseph Weissman and published on Sunday, September 30, 2007 at 5:27 pm. See: http://fractalontology.wordpress.com/2007/09/30/nietzsche-and-the-unconscious-ethics-desire-politics/

63 Jung, C. G. *Memories, Dreams, Reflections*. Op. Cit., P. 200.

64 Ibid. PP. 170-199.

65 Jung, C. G. (1988). *Nietzsche's Zarathustra: Notes of the Seminar Given in 1934-1939*. Ed. Jarrett, J. L. Princeton. Princeton University Press.

66 Ibid. P. 184 ff.

67 Kerenyi, K. (1990). *Hermes: Guide of Souls*. Op. Cit. P. 88.

68 Heidegger, M. Tr. Hertz, P. D. (1971). *On the Way to Language*. San Francisco. Harper San Francisco. Pp. 73-75.

69 Op. Cit. Pp. 187-197.

70 Hillman, James; Shamdasani, Sonu (2013-08-26). *Lament of the Dead: Psychology After Jung's Red Book*. W. W. Norton & Company. Kindle Edition. Location 81.

71 Giegerich, W. (2010). "Liber Novis, that is, The New Bible, A First Analysis of C. G. Jung's Red Book". *Spring 83*, 361-413. Pp. 371 ff.

72 See also: Giegerich, W. (2013). *The Flight into the Unconscious*. New Orleans. Spring Journal Books. P.236ff.

73 Giegerich, W. (2010). *Liber Novis, that is, The New Bible, A First Analysis of C. G. Jung's Red Book*. Op. Cit. Pp. 391-2 ff.

74 Jung, C. G. (G. A. Adler, Ed., & R. F. Hull, Trans.). (1975). *C. G. Jung Letters (Vols. 2 (1951-1960)*. London: Routledge and Kegan Paul. P. 51.

[75] Jung, C. G. (R. F. Hull, tr.). (1977). *The Collected Works of C. G. Jung (2nd ed., Vol. 11)*. Princeton: Princeton University Press. Par. 233.

[76] Jung, C. G. (G. A. Adler, Ed., & R. F. Hull, Tr.). (1975). *C. G. Jung Letters (Vols. 2 (1951-1960))*. London: Routledge and Kegan Paul. P. 525. With thanks to Wolfgang Giegerich. See *The Flight into the Unconscious*. Op. Cit.

[77] Giegerich, W. (2010). *Liber Novis, that is, The New Bible, A First Analysis of C. G. Jung's Red Book*. Op. Cit. Pp. 367 ff.

[78] Interestingly, Philip K. Dick also "tears fantasy and truth apart" in a move that violates Giegerich's conception of art. Dick writes: "I am a fictionalizing philosopher, not a novelist; my novel & story-writing ability is employed as a means to formulate my perception. The core of my writing is not art but truth." Found in: Lawrence Sutin. *Divine Invasions: A Life of Philip K. Dick* (Kindle Locations 158-159). Kindle Edition. I said that Giegerich is basing his criticism of this "violation" on his well-established conception of art (he cites Dante's *Divine Comedy* as a counter example). But I believe that these moves by Jung and Dick are also hints towards a new definition of art, one based on the interpenetration of fictional reality with empirical reality with which both men were intimately involved their entire lives. To achieve this, they have to negate or downgrade all previous *definitions* of art (as *now* having nothing to do with truth).

[79] Ibid. Pp. 365-6.

[80] See http://www.ispdi.org for a introduction to Wolfgang Giegerich's psychology.

[81] Giegerich, W. (2005). *The Neurosis of Psychology*. New Orleans. Spring Journal Books.

[82] See Giegerich. *Liber Novis, that is, The New Bible, A First Analysis of C. G. Jung's Red Book*. Op. Cit. P.364.

[83] Quoted in: Lockhart, R. A. (1987). *Psyche Speaks: A Jungian Approach to Self and World*. Wilmette: Chiron. P. 79

[84] Heidegger, M. *On the Way to Language*. Op. Cit. P. 122-3.

[85] I put "Descartes" in quotes to signify a philosophy, or a status of consciousness where "inwardness" is felt to be "in" us, while nature became an object, without an "inner".

[86] I have used the word, "participation" to mean the unity of Being and reflection, after Owen Barfield's terms "final participation", or "philosophical double-vision". See: Barfield, O. (1957). *Saving the Appearances*. Op. Cit. And also: Barfield, O. (1997). *The Rediscovery of Meaning*. San Rafael. California. Pp. 24 ff.

[87] Ibid.

[88] Philosophical double-vision is a concept that only points us to the experience. It is not a concept that the phenomenon has taught us. I.e., it is not a word that belongs to, and "says", the new world as can be seen by its awkward construction. Barfield tries to "say" the new world from a stance that the new world has overcome and left behind. See: Barfield, O. (1997). *The Rediscovery of Meaning*. Op. Cit. Pp. 32-33.

[89] For a fuller discussion of my own experience with philosophical double-vision see: Woodcock, J. C. (2011). *The Imperative*. Op. Cit. Pp. 38 ff. In this particular experience which I call a dream-vision, a poem burst forth from within the dream. This was a moment of inception or Ereignis which is the beginning of languaging a new world.

[90] Jackson, P. and Lethem, J. (Eds) (2011). *The Exegesis of Philip K. Dick*. New York. Houghton Mifflin Harcourt. P. xii.

[91] Sutin, L. (1989). *Divine Invasions: A Life of Philip K. Dick*. New York. Carroll and Graf. Also see the Introduction to *Exegesis*. Op. Cit.

[92] Borges, J. L. (1962). "Tlön, Uqbar, Orbis, Tertuis". *Labyrinths. Selected Stories and Other Writings*.

[93] http://en.wikipedia.org/wiki/Tl%C3%B6n,_Uqbar,_Orbis_Tertius.

[94] Lewis, C. S. (2012, 11 29). *C. S. Lewis Lectures on the Novels of Charles Williams*. Retrieved from YouTube: https://www.youtube.com/watch?v=Z5w134gYz04.

[95] Williams, C. (2003). *The Place of the Lion*. Vancouver. Regent College Publishing. P. 170.

[96] Woodcock, J. C. (2012). *Making of a Man: Initiation through the Divine Mother*. Bloomington. IUniverse. From the Introduction.

[97] Jackson, P. and Lethem, J. (Eds) (2011). *The Exegesis of Philip K. Dick*. Op. Cit. From the Introduction.

[98] Woodcock, J.C. (2013). *Overcoming Solidity: World Crisis and the New Nature*. Bloomington. iUniverse. Pp. 33 ff.

[99] See my doctoral thesis, (Project Demonstrating Excellence) which I finished in ten days, the culmination of my heuristic research and a description of my own breakdown: http://www.lighthousedownunder.com/doctoral_work.htm.

[100] This curious construction, "fictional reality *wants* . . ." is also expressed by Lockhart as "the dream's desire". In this way we can see a reversal in the engine of desire, from us desiring, to us being the object of desire, where "something else" wants something of us. This is mirrored in my experience of my "Star Sister" as well as C. G. Jung's erotic/fearful encounter with Salome in *The Red Book* and Philip K. Dick's encounters with the "dark-haired girl". In alchemy desire belongs to the operation of *coagulatio*, in which spiritual reality coagulates into earthly life, or incarnates.

[101] Graves, R. (1994). *The White Goddess: A Historical Grammar of Poetic Myth*. New York. The Noonday Press. P. 14.

[102] Wordsworth's poetry is exemplary of this pervasive mood of loss and nostalgia, known as Romanticism.

[103] Here I offer one of my own visions in which I was shown that the transformation of the lived-world is in fact Her own doing. See my book: Woodcock, J. C. (2012). *Animal Soul*. Bloomington, iUniverse. P. 43 ff. This gets to the very mystery and *telos* of Being.

[104] Op. Cit. P. 444.

[105] Tolstoy, N. (1989). *The Coming of the King: A Novel of Merlin*. London. Bantam Books. P.175.

[106] Woodcock, J. C. (2013). *Overcoming Solidity*. Op. Cit. P. 27 ff.

[107] Op. Cit.

[108] This and other encounters are discussed in my book, *The Imperative*. Op. Cit. They all have the character of fictional reality interpenetrating with empirical reality. For many years I had no idea how to convey this perplexing matter. It bordered on madness as many voice hearers know.

[109] Adler, G., & Jaffe, A. (Eds.). (1975). *C. G. Jung Letters* (Vols. 2 (1951-1961)). (R. F. Hull, Trans.) London: Routledge & Kegan Paul, Ltd. P. 590.

110 Hillman, J. (1994). *Healing Fiction.* Dallas. Spring Publications, Inc.

111 Ibid. Chapter: *The Empirical Fiction.* P12 ff.

112 Ibid. P. 25.

113 See: Giegerich, W. (2010). *The Soul Always Thinks.* New Orleans. Spring Journal Books. Pp. 73 ff. for a fuller treatment of his criticism of Hillman's project.

114 Giegerich, W. (2001). *The Soul's Logical Life.* Berlin. Peter Lang.

115 Giegerich, W. (2007). *Technology and the Soul.* New Orleans. Spring Journal Books.

116 Barfield, O. (1957). *Saving the Appearances.* Op. Cit. Pp. 145-146.

117 I wrote this piece during my doctoral program in 1998. It also appears in my book: Woodcock, J. C. (2013). *Living in Uncertainty Living with Spirit.* Bloomington. iUniverse.

118 For a fuller account, see my book, *The Imperative.* Op. Cit.

119 Marlowe, S. (1995). *The Lighthouse at the End of the World.* New York. Plume.

120 This story, "From Dream to World" is found in my book *Living in Uncertainty Living with Spirit.* Op. Cit.

121 See my essay: "Year of the Peacock", also found in my book, *Living in Uncertainty Living with Spirit.* Op. Cit.

122 Ibid. P. 207.

123 See my book, *The Imperative.* Op. Cit.

124 Emerson, R. W. *The Over-Soul.* Digital Emerson: A Collective Archive. http://digitalemerson.wsulibs.wsu.edu/exhibits/show/about.

125 Oliver, M. (1990). *House of Light.* Boston. Beacon Press.

126 Marlowe, S. (1995). *The Lighthouse at the End of the World.* Op.Cit. Pp. 212-213.

127 Lockhart, R. A. (1987). *Psyche Speaks.* Wilmette. Chiron Pub. P. 50. This book is based on Lockhart's inaugural lectures in 1982, sponsored by the C. G. Jung Foundation for Analytical Psychology, Inc. in New York. The purpose of these lectures was to make an original contribution to Jungian Psychology.

128 With thanks to the poetry of Machado.

129 See Dreyfus, H. L. (1995). *Being-in-the-World: A Commentary of Heidegger's Being and Time, Division 1.* Cambridge. The MIT Press.

130 With thanks to Wolfgang Giegerich for this conception: See Giegerich, W. *Soul Violence*. Op. Cit. Pp. 382 ff.

131 TIME. (27/01/2007). *Mind and Body Special Issue*. Vol. 169. No. 5.

132 Haig, S. (2007). *The Power of Hope*. TIME. Op. Cit. Pp. 118-119.

133 The Angel of History. See: Benjamin, W. (ed. Arendt, H. Tr. Zohn, H.). (1988). "Thesis on the Philosophy of History". *Illuminations: Essays and Reflections*. New York, Schocken Books.

134 William Wordsworth: *Ode, Intimations of Immortality from Recollections of Early Childhood*.

135 See my book, *The Imperative*, Op. Cit., for a fuller account of this period of my life.

136 *Last of the Mohicans*. (1992). Music by Enya.

137 McKennitt, L. (1994). *The Mask and the Mirror*. Quinlan Road.

138 When I finally travelled to my father's hometown in England, my sister showed me his old haunts and work places. To my considerable surprise, she showed me a small lighthouse that he had built single-handedly.

139 Woodcock, J. C. (2013) *Making of a Man: Initiation through the Divine Mother*. Bloomington. iUniverse.

140 See Jung's image of "suspension", p. 37 ff.

141 I compose such a "Book of Quotations" in my book: Woodcock, J. C. (2013). *UR-image*. Bloomington. iUniverse.

142 Benjamin, W. (1988). *Illuminations: Essays and Reflections*. Op. Cit.

143 Grimm, J. a. (2007, April 12). *Household Tales*. Retrieved from Wikipedia: http://en.wikipedia.org/wiki/The_Valiant_Little_Tailor.

144 Kingsley, P. (2003). *Reality*. Inverness: Golden Sufi Cente. P. 90.

145 Ibid. Pp. 91, 94, and 437.

146 Ibid. P. 485.

147 See my Introduction.

148 Barfield, O. (1957). *Saving the Appearances*. Op. Cit. Pp. 145-146.

149 See: A Companion to Heidegger (Blackwell Companions to Philosophy, Vol. 29) (Kindle Location 7052). Kindle Edition for a full discussion of Heidegger's conception of the *telos* of history, a concept that points to a sense of completion. As each new epoch or life-world comes into being, so too, history re-sets itself in the sense that all the questions asked in the previous epoch are not so much answered, as

made irrelevant. We can see this process in Jung's understanding too, expressed as the movement from the Piscean age to the Aquarian age. The problem of the opposites, e. g. good and evil, which were so vital and alive in the former age, seem now simply to have disappeared. But underlying these epochal transformations is a telos of history, a *becoming*, moving toward completion, according to Heidegger.

[150] See, for example: Williams, C. (2003). *The Place of the Lion.* Vancouver. Regent College Publishing.

[151] For a fuller account of this moment, see: Woodcock, J. C. *The Imperative.* Bloomington. iUniverse. P. 43 ff.

[152] King, S. (2009). *UR.* Storyville, LLC. Kindle Edition.

[153] See Introduction.

[154] King, S. (2009). *UR.* Storyville, LLC. Kindle Edition. (Kindle Locations 631-642).

[155] Woodcock, J. C. (2013). *Ur-image.* Bloomington. iUniverse. From the back cover.

[156] Lockhart, R. A. *Psyche Speaks.* Op. Cit. P. 19.

[157] Kerenyi, K. (1990). *Hermes: Guide of Souls.* Dallas. Spring Publications Inc.

[158] Ibid. P. 72.

[159] Giegerich, W. (2012). *What is Soul?* New Orleans. Spring Journal Books. P. 264.

[160] Kerenyi, K. Op. Cit. P. 88.

[161] Graves, R. Op. Cit. Chapter: *Dog, Roebuck and Lapwing.* P. 49 ff.

[162] Heidegger, M. (1982). On *the Way to Language.* New York. Harper and Row.

[163] I had used a form of Hermeneutics in my doctoral program so I was already familiar with the research method but this was something different. I was, as I said, on the trail of a quarry. Hermes was at work and something was about to be disclosed to me. I could *sense* it!

[164] Ibid. P. 30.

[165] See above in the Introduction.

[166] Dasein is that being who seeks to understand Being, and constitutes our essential nature or our way of being which is only disclosed to us by the way we cope in the world, the way we *comport* ourselves.

[167] For a full discussion of worlds, see: Dreyfus, H. L. (1995). *Being-in-the-World. A Companion to Heidegger's Being and Time, Division 1.* Cambridge. MIT Press.

[168] See my books, *The Imperative, Transformation of the World* for a fuller account of my ordeal. Op. Cit.

[169] About half-way through these lectures, I discovered that they had been removed by the contributor. I felt robbed. They were gone! But a quick search of the Internet found the entire series, available to the public, at: https://archive.org/details/Philosophy_185_Fall_2007_UC_Berkeley.